Constructing Knowledge Together

Constructing Knowledge Together

Classrooms as
Centers
of Inquiry
and
Literacy

Gordon Wells and Gen Ling Chang-Wells

Heinemann
Portsmouth, NH

Heinemann Educational Books, Inc.
361 Hanover Street
Portsmouth, NH 03801−3959
Offices and agents throughout the world

With the exception of chapter 1, the chapters that make up this volume have already
appeared in print, in whole or in part. The authors wish to thank the following
publishers for permission to reprint.

Chapter 2. Talk for learning and teaching. By G. Wells. In M. Hayhoe and S. Parker,
eds. *Language and Literacy*. Open University Press, in press.
Chapter 3. "The literate potential of collaborative talk." By G. L. Chang and G. Wells.
In M. MacLure, T. Phillips and A. Wilkinson, eds. *Oracy Matters*, pp. 95−109. Open
University Press, 1988.
Chapter 4. "Language in the classroom: Literacy and collaborative talk." *Language
and Education, 3(4)*, 251−73, 1989.
Chapter 5. "Creating classroom communities of literate thinkers." By G. L. Chang,
G. Wells and A. Maher. In S. Sharan, ed. *Cooperative Learning: Theory and
Research*, pp. 95−121. Praeger Publishers, 1990.
Chapter 6. Concepts of literacy and their consequences for children's potential as
learners. By G. L. Chang and G. Wells. In S. P. Norris and L. M. Phillips, eds.
Foundations of Literacy Policy in Canada, pp. 207−26. Copyright 1991 by Detselig
Enterprises Ltd.
Chapter 7. Talk about text: Where literacy is learned and taught. *Curriculum
Inquiry*, 20(4), 369−405. Copyright 1990 by The Ontario Institute for Studies in
Education. Published by John Wiley & Sons, Inc.

Library of Congress Cataloging-in-Publication Data

Wells, C. Gordon.
    Constructing knowledge together: classrooms as centers of inquiry
and literacy/Gordon Wells and Gen Ling Chang-Wells.
        p.   cm.
    Includes bibliographical references (p.) and index.
    ISBN 0−435−08731−2
    1. Learning—Longitudinal studies. 2. Language and education—
-Ontario—Toronto—Longitudinal studies. 3. Intercultural
education—Ontario—Toronto—Longitudinal studies. I. Chang-Wells,
Gen Ling. II. Title.
LB1060.W45 1992
370.15'23—dc20   92−11630
                                                             CIP

Printed in the United States of America on acid free paper
92   93   94   95   96   9   8   7   6   5   4   3   2   1

Contents

Acknowledgments

The papers collected in this volume grew out of a research project carried out in four schools in the city of Toronto between 1985 and 1989. The project, entitled "Language and Learning: Effecting Change Through Collaborative Research in Multilingual Schools" was funded by grants from the Ontario Ministry of Education, the Ontario Institute for Studies in Education (under the Transfer Grant from the Ministry of Education), and from the Toronto Board of Education. I wish to express my gratitude to these institutions for their financial support. However, I must make it clear that the views expressed in these chapters are those of the authors and not necessarily those of the funding agencies.

Many people contributed to the success of the project: the seventy-two children whose classroom experiences we observed; their parents and teachers, who both welcomed us into their homes and classrooms and discussed the significance of our observations with us; the school and central administrative staff, who helped us to overcome the logistical problems inherent in carrying out a large-scale longitudinal study. I should also like to thank the following people for their unfailing support and encouragement: Don Rutledge, Associate Director (Curriculum), and Freda Appleyard, Head of the Language Study Centre, of the Toronto Board of Education; Bob Barton and Sue Alderson, education officers at the Ontario Ministry of Education; and Angela Hildyard, Assistant Director (Field Studies and Research) of the Ontario Institute for Studies in Education.

For all or part of the duration of the project, the following members of the research team were responsible for the collection, transcription, and analysis of the data. The research officers were: William Baird, Barbara Bell, Marion Blake, Gen Ling Chang, Peter Dimitrijevic, Ilda Januario, Alice Huynh, Mei Lian Lam, Anna Paliouri, Jack Pledger, Sandra Schecter, Myriam Shechter, Frank Tramposch, William McKellin; graduate students included: Barbara Barter, Margaret Cameron, David Coe, Maria Esquillo, Brigitte Harris, Gail Heald-Taylor, Judy Hunter, Margaret Joyce, Beverley Kirkland, Francis Mangubhai, Emilia Rivas-Arraiz, Bairu Suim, Elizabeth Strauss, Tony Xerri; and the administrative assistants were JoAnne

Squires and Rikki Hortian. I am most grateful to all of them for their dedicated and untiring effort—often in the face of considerable difficulty—that culminated in the preparation and presentation of the final report of the project, *Language and Learning: Learners, Teachers and Researchers at Work*, in four volumes, to be published by the Ontario Ministry of Education.

Based on the work reported there, the chapters that make up this volume describe and reflect on some of the collaborative inquiries undertaken with teachers in the participating schools. To these teachers, and their children, I owe a special debt of gratitude for the way they welcomed us into their classroom communities and for the insights we gained in the course of our work together.

I should also like to thank the many other people from whom I have learned through the dialogues of various kinds I have had during the preparation of this book: my graduate students, my colleagues, and the many people from different parts of the world who contribute to the XLCHC electronic mail network organized by Michael Cole at the University of California, San Diego. I should particularly like to thank the following: Dave Pratt, for allowing me to use, in chapter 2, an episode recorded in his classroom, and Allan MacKinnon for discussing the transcript with me; David Booth and Glenn Humphreys for their helpful comments on earlier drafts of chapter 2 and Michael Cole, Maggie Lampert, David Olson, and Robert Serpell on drafts of chapter 7.

Finally, in the writing of all these chapters, I have benefited enormously from the ideas and suggestions of Gen Ling Chang-Wells, my colleague and partner in all aspects of the project. Several of the chapters we wrote in collaboration and, for all the others, she was an important influence on both the content and the form. A constant source of inspiration and support, she has done more than anyone to enable this project to come to fruition.

Conventions of Transcription

Layout   Each new utterance starts on a new line and, if more than one line is required to complete the utterance, continuation lines are indented. Utterances are numbered sequentially from the beginning of the episode for easy reference.

—   Incomplete utterances or false starts are shown with a dash, e.g., "Well—er—"

·   Pauses are indicated with a period. In the case of long pauses, the number of periods corresponds to the number of seconds of pause, e.g., "Yes .. I do."

?!   These punctuation marks are used to mark utterances judged to have an interrogative or exclamatory intention.

CAPS   Capitals are used for words spoken with emphasis, e.g., "I really LOVE painting."

<>   Angle brackets are used to enclose words or phrases about which the transcriber felt uncertain.

*   Passages that are impossible to transcribe are shown with asterisks, one for each word judged to have been spoken e.g., "I'll go ***."

——   When two speakers speak at once, the overlapping portions of their utterances are underlined.

(Gloss)   Where it is judged necessary, an interpretation of what was said or of the way in which it was said is given in parentheses.

Introduction
Collaborative Research in
Multilingual Schools

The Voices of the Children

One morning in the early summer of 1987 as I was working in my office, the telephone rang. The caller was one of the teachers in whose classroom we were carrying out regular observations as part of a longitudinal study of children's language and learning. However, the call was not about any of the routine matters associated with the organization of the project. Instead, the teacher was asking me to pay a visit to her classroom that afternoon. "And please bring the video camera with you," she asked.

As this was not a scheduled visit, I wasn't sure what to expect when I made my way that afternoon to her combined grade three and four classroom in a school in downtown Toronto. But it didn't take me long to discover. Even before I entered the room, I could hear, above the sound of children's voices engaged in animated conversation, the plaintive "peep, peep" of newly hatched chicks. However, the sound was not coming from the incubator, which I saw as soon as I entered the room. This contained only a couple of eggs that had so far failed to hatch. Instead, the peeping was coming from every direction—from the center of each of the groups of children, who were working at desks, on the floor in the carpeted area, and in every corner of the room. "This is Junior, our little friend," said Amy, holding up one of the chicks for me to see. "We're trying to find out whether it's a boy or a girl."

Nearby, Marilda and her friend are sitting at a desk covered in newspaper. In the center is a pan balance, in one of the pans of which sits a quite well-developed chick, which occasionally has to be restrained as it tries to clamber out. Marilda is adding weights to the other pan until they balance; her friend is writing down the result: "78 grams." "That's because he's one day older," observes Marilda, referring to the increase since the previous day.

To one side, on the floor, three boys are busy with what looks like a pile of junk—cardboard boxes, sheets of newspaper, and a plentiful supply of adhesive tape. They also have a collection of electrical supplies—batteries, bulbs, switches, and wire—which they are connecting together in and around the structure they are making. Somewhere in the center of this another of the chicks can be heard, although not seen. "I'll turn on the switch and see if it lights up," says Salvatore. It does. They are making a house for their chick, they inform me.

When I finally locate the teacher, she is kneeling on the floor, gently stroking one of the chicks that Brian is holding while two of his friends are drawing what they see. "It's funny how they flick their heads," the teacher observes, "have you noticed that?" Then, as she looks with them at the claws, she adds "Notice the marks on its toes. Have you people measured the toes?"

Measuring the toes is apparently what Barbara and Uma are doing. They have a saucer of water-based paint and a large sheet of clean paper. Uma picks up a chick, dips its claws in the paint, and sets it down on the paper. It leaves a trail of blue clawprints. "Chick painting," Barbara laughs to Uma, and repeats the process, starting the chick at a different point on the paper.

By now, the teacher has joined another group. They have been experimenting with two chicks to find out what they are most likely to peck at. "They're quiet when they're both together," reports Joao. "If you take one away, the other will start pecking." "That's interesting," remarks the teacher. "How are you recording what you observe?"

A few minutes later, the bell rings for recess. While the children are out in the yard, I look around the classroom, noting the sheets of chart paper pinned to the walls on which are written some of the questions they have decided to investigate: "How do chicks drink?" "Where are their ears?" "When do they peep?" "What kind of things will s/he go for (peck at)?" On another sheet of paper have been noted some of the changes they have observed: "a bump on the chest," "egg tooth gone," "weighs more," "growing feathers of different colors."

Next to these sheets of paper, arranged under the heading "What can we observe and learn about the chicks?" is another sheet headed

"Adoptive Parents." As I am looking at this in some surprise, the teacher brings me a beautifully handwritten document. It is a Certificate of Adoption that a group of girls have drawn up.

Adoption Paper

I swear to the holy
Bible that I will feed and nourish
this chick through
poor and health
As long as we will
be together.

NAME OF ADOPTOR

APPROVAL OF *CHICK*

CRACKER

Photo of Chick

Signature of parent

Expires Date. May 27.

As we are enjoying the echoes of the marriage vows to be heard in this document — presumably remembered from a family wedding that one of the group had attended — I report a conversation I had overheard a few minutes earlier: several children had been speculating on why one of the chicks seemed to follow one particular child, and it seemed that they were spontaneously moving towards Conrad Lorenz's theory of imprinting. The children begin to come back into the classroom, and I return to my position behind the video camera.

The last part of the afternoon is to be devoted to a sharing session — a regular activity in this classroom — when the children will have the opportunity, as the teacher announces, "to share with your friends the things you have been studying, what you have learned, and what you're trying to find out." After a period of preparation, the children gather on the rug and the teacher asks for volunteers to talk about where they have got to in their projects.

João is one of the first to be chosen. He picks up his papers and goes to sit in the speaker's chair, facing the rest of the class. He waits for silence. Then, holding up a piece of paper, he explains: "This is Cheep's graph. I recorded Monday and Tuesday. Monday was a little hard because we had to divide with the beans and with the grams." With this introduction, João goes on to read from his learning log. He wants to read all his entries but, as time is short, the teacher asks him to read only his entry for today.

> Yesterday was Monday. And he weighed 73 gr. but today he has only gained 2 gr. So he weighs 75 gr. We know that Cheep is going to be a rooster because he has something on his head and that is called a comb. The comb is small now because he is small, too. We have a paper to record how heavy he is. We can do lots more like a graph for the size, and one for the height. When Cheep is on a table that is cold he goes to the washroom and when he's warm and feeling good he doesn't go to the washroom. This morning we recorded the sounds of the chicks. We used lots of chicks to see if there is a difference.

Immediately after he finishes, a number of children ask questions: "Is there a difference?" "What do you mean by the difference — tall, short?" João replies that he was trying to discover whether there was a difference in their voices, whether some were higher and others lower. "Can you tell one chick from another by their voices?" asks the teacher. Smiling mischievously, he replies that one of the chicks didn't peep so they couldn't tell. The last question for which there is time is about the comb. João explains that you can tell it's a rooster because, even when they're young, rooster chicks have bigger combs than girl chicks.

When Marilda's turn comes, she too has interesting information to share. "My chick, Jumpy, is a fast runner", she announces, reading from her log. "It beat the others in a race. It has also begun to grow feathers." However, as she is uncertain of its sex, she punctiliously refers to it throughout as "he or she." When Marilda has finished reading, she also shows her graph of the chick's increasing weight ("in fives," she says in an aside). Finally, she holds up two sheets of paper on which there are patterns of paint. These, she claims, show that Jumpy has larger claws than one of the younger chicks.

Salvatore, the last child to share on this occasion, has something very different to show. Like many of the other children, he has been concerned that the newly hatched chicks should not catch cold and, with a couple of friends, he has constructed the house that I saw him working on earlier for the chick that they have adopted. However, not content to line the box with warm material, as some of the other children have done, he has drawn upon his knowledge of electric circuits to incorporate both lighting and central heating. As he stands facing the group, he proudly shows how to switch the light on and off and, in answer to questions, explains some of the principles involved in the wiring.

At that point, it was time to end the sharing session. As the children placed their chairs on top of their desks, packed their tote bags, and left the classroom for the day, the teacher began to tell me about some of the unexpected directions this project had taken.

Her intention, she said, had been that the chicks should hatch at the beginning of the week, and she had set up the incubator accordingly. However, nature had not cooperated and some of the eggs had begun to hatch at the end of the previous week. While the children had watched with fascination as the chicks pecked at their shells to create an opening and emerged, bedraggled, into the daylight, the conversation had quite naturally centered on their apparent helplessness and their need for warmth and protection. Somebody had suggested making houses for them and, within minutes, the idea of adoption had been raised. Groups quickly formed and, as each new chick emerged, it was adopted and named, and subsequently marked with a colored felt-tip pen so that it could be distinguished from the others. All these ideas had come from the children, the teacher added, and the project had taken off under their direction in ways that far exceeded the more limited aims she had had in mind.

As we talked about the ways in which children are constantly surprising their teachers with their novel solutions to problems — and even with the problems themselves — she went on to give two further examples, both arising from this unit on chicks. The first concerned the measurement of weight. In order to track the growth of their chicks, the children had initially used the simple pan balances that were part of the equipment of the classroom. Placing their chick in one pan, they had added beans to the other until the two pans balanced and then counted the number of beans that had been required. Quite quickly the numbers had become rather large, and so the teacher had borrowed a set of gram weights from a colleague. However, this had posed a problem: the first measurements of the chicks' weights had been recorded in beans and the later ones in grams; how could the two sets of measurements be compared? (João had alluded to this problem, I now realized, in the preamble to his report at sharing time.) As they discussed this problem, a solution was proposed by one of the children: what was needed was a conversion chart. And so, by balancing beans against gram weights, such a chart was eventually produced and the earlier weights in beans were converted to weights in grams, providing a great deal of meaningful work on division in the process.

The second surprise was also of a mathematical kind. In order to display the increasing weight of the chicks, the teacher had introduced the idea of making a bar chart. And, taking a large sheet of graph paper, she had begun to demonstrate, using one square to represent one gram. However, since the weights to be represented were already in excess of fifty grams, she quickly reached the top of the first sheet of paper and started on a second. Clearly, as some of the children saw, they had another problem: as the chicks grew, the height of the bar representing the weight on successive days would require three, or even more, sheets of paper added end to end. As a result, the graphs were going to be too big to display on the classroom walls. Once again, a solution came from the children: instead of each square representing one gram, a square could be used to represent a larger, but fixed, number of grams, such as five or ten. And so the idea of scaling was reinvented. It was this convention that Marilda had drawn attention to in her aside, "in fives," when showing her graph to the rest of the class in the sharing session earlier in the afternoon.

Although not mentioned by the teacher — probably because they were regular and taken-for-granted practices in this classroom — there were other aspects of the children's ways of working that I had been struck by. First, there was the evidence, displayed on the walls, that the questions they were investigating had come from the children as well as from the teacher. João's observation of the conditions under which Cheep "went to the washroom" is a case in point. The question that his observation answered did not figure in any of the written lists. Secondly, I noted the eagerness with which children asked questions in sharing-time, requesting further elaborations and explanations from the presenters on the topics about which they were recognized to be the experts. I also noted how, as texts to support their reports to the rest of the class on work in progress, the writing that the children were doing in their learning logs had taken on a purpose that made it more than a task to be carried out to satisfy the teacher. Finally, I was struck by the easy way in which the children moved between doing, talking, and writing, with each activity supporting and complementing the others, and by the connections the children were making between different ways of representing information — in drawings, graphs, and writing — thereby bridging the chasms between language, math, science, and social studies that so often lead to a fragmentation of knowledge as it is constructed in school.

The Research Project: Aims and Methods

I have described this afternoon observation in some detail because, although not typical, it provides an excellent introduction to some of the major themes of the rest of the book. It also gives a good idea of the sort of data that the project set out to collect.

First, the children themselves. In this classroom, as in all four schools in which our research was carried out, the majority of the children came from homes in which a language other than English was the dominant mode of communication. In fact, in this particular classroom, more than ninety percent of the children spoke a language, or languages, other than English with the adults who conversed with them at home.[1] Such children face a much more demanding task at school than their monolingual English-speaking peers. Not only do they have to master the skills and subject-related content of the school curriculum, but they simultaneously have to learn the language in which this curriculum is presented as well as the ground rules of classroom interaction (Edwards and Mercer 1987), which may be quite different from those that, based on their own schooling in a different culture, their parents have prepared them to expect.

Not surprisingly, these children from ethnolinguistic minority backgrounds tend to lag behind their monolingual peers on criterion-based or standardized measures of achievement — at least in the first few years of schooling. This lag has led to a disproportionately high incidence of children from these groups being assessed as having learning problems when, in many cases, their real problem is not an inability to learn so much as an exclusion from the opportunities provided for learning by virtue of their difficulty in communicating with teachers who do not understand their predicament (Cummins 1984). One of the main aims of our longitudinal study, therefore, was to try to gain a better understanding of the way in which such children experienced the opportunities and demands of the curriculum, as presented to them in classrooms in which English was the sole medium of instruction, and how their different experiences were related to their progress and achievement.

After consultation with the Toronto Board of Education, in whose jurisdiction we planned to carry out the research, we decided to work with children from four ethnolinguistic groups: Chinese, Greek, Portuguese, and English. Four schools were approached that served communities with the appropriate ethnic mix and, on the advice of the teachers, we selected six children at each of three grade levels in each school (kindergarten, grade two, and grade four), such that in two schools the sample at each grade level consisted of Greek, Chinese, and English-speaking children, and in the other two schools of Portuguese, Chinese and English-speaking children. Then, over the next three years (from 1985 through 1988), each child was observed three times during the course of each school year, with the observation lasting a complete session, either morning or afternoon. As there were six children to be observed in each class, there was a total of eighteen observations in each class-room in each year. During the observations, the field researcher kept a continuous running record of the child's activities, typing the field notes directly into a lap-top computer. Using a radio microphone, the child's conversation was simultaneously recorded on a tape recorder, selected episodes of which were then transcribed for subsequent analysis. At some point in the session, if possible, the researcher also carried out a coinvestigation with the child about the work in which he or she was engaged.

These observations, together with tests administered in November and June of each year and interviews with the children, their parents, and their teachers, provided the data for comparisons between the four groups and for case studies of individual children from each of the ethnolinguistic minority groups.[2]

A second reason for presenting the observation of the chick project at some length is the set of features that distinguish the approach to curriculum that it exemplifies from what was happening in some of the other classrooms that we observed. These include:

- the recognition of the active nature of learning, manifested in opportunities for learners to set their own goals, plan and carry out the activities necessary to achieve them, evaluate the consequences, and present the outcomes of their work to an interested audience of peers;

- the recognition of the social nature of learning, manifested in the encouragement of collaboration between learners in all aspects of their work and in the guidance and assistance provided by the teacher through conferences with individuals and groups while tasks are in progress as well as when they have been completed;

- the recognition of the affective foundation of thinking and learning, manifested in the positive value accorded to empathy, curiosity, caring, and risk taking;

- the recognition of the holistic nature of learning, manifested in the spontaneous integration of information and strategies from the domains of language, science, social studies, and mathematics in the interests of action that is purposeful and meaningful;

- the recognition of the central role of language both as the medium through which learning takes place and as the means for collaboration and integration, manifested in the encouragement of learners' purposeful use of their linguistic resources, both spoken and written, as tools for thinking, cooperating, and communicating in relation to the tasks that they undertake.

One way of describing a classroom in which these principles guide the manner in which the curriculum is enacted is "a community of literate thinkers." And one of the aims of our project was to encourage the development of such communities. The question that faced us, however, was how to set about it.

Most educational research can be seen as belonging to one of two types. The first, which is typified by large-scale observational studies, attempts to describe what is actually happening in classrooms. This was certainly the approach that I adopted in my previous work in the Bristol Study, "Language at Home and at School," in which a representative sample of children was followed from the very beginnings of their language development to the end of the elementary stage of their education.[3] However, whether the ultimate purpose of such research is to explain what is observed or to evaluate it against some notional ideal, the emphasis is on describing what "is".

The problem with this approach is that, at best, it presents a picture of exemplary current practice for emulation by others and, at worst, it castigates dedicated and hard-working teachers for putting into practice the educational theories that formed the basis of their training but that are now judged to be misguided or inadequate. In neither case, however, does this sort of descriptive research provide much assistance to those teachers who would like to change.

The second type of educational research is perhaps better called development, using the second of the two terms in the traditional category of Research and Development. This approach is typified by intervention studies that attempt to introduce some new curriculum material or an improved approach to pedagogy or classroom management. Almost invariably, the intervention is planned by "experts" outside the classroom, and the new material or approach is presented as a package to be implemented according to the prescriptions of its designer. Here the emphasis is on making changes to what is, in order to achieve what "ought" to be the case, according to the beliefs and values of the originator of the change.

However this approach, too, is fraught with problems and rarely proves successful (Fullan 1982). For, although there is a clear commitment to the improvement of practice and, in many cases, quite intensive training in how to implement the proposed change, two essential elements are missing: the grounding of change in what is, in the sense of the specific cultural and historical context of particular classrooms, and the active involvement of the individual teachers in deciding what sort of changes to make and how best to make them.

In terms of the contrast that I have set up, then, neither type of research is likely to be successful in creating improved learning opportunities for students. If it is insufficient simply to describe what is, it is equally ineffective to intervene to try to impose what an external agent judges ought to be done.

But there is an alternative, which may have a greater chance of success. And that is to encourage teachers to start from their own particular circumstances in an exploration of what they and their students "might" be able to achieve. By formulating their own alternatives, trying them out in practice, and selecting those that they judge to be successful, teachers can act as agents in effecting change, even when the overall goals are prescribed by local or national policymakers.[4]

Any educational change, whether of curriculum content or of classroom practice, involves teachers in a process of learning. The advantage of the third approach, therefore, is that, not only does it make teachers' learning central to the process of effecting change, but it also attempts to create conditions for learning that are based on the very same principles that were presented above as the basis for effective learning in the classroom.

Initiating Collaborative Action Research

This, then was the approach we attempted to adopt. Through various types of collaborative inquiry with those teachers who were willing to take up our invitation, and through meetings at which we shared the work we were doing, we tried to create a community of literate thinkers whose goal was to improve the learning opportunities for the children that they taught.

My third reason for introducing João, Marilda, and Salvatore, and for describing in some detail the ways in which they were learning in their work on the newly hatched chicks, was that their teacher was one of those who became involved in a collaborative inquiry. In fact, at the point when she invited me to visit her chick laboratory, she had already begun to formulate the question she wanted to address.

That she had already adopted the stance of a "reflective" (Schön 1983) or "thoughtful" (Atwell 1989) practitioner was apparent from her comments in our discussion at the end of my visit. Some of these concerned the events that had surprised her, such as the children's creation of the chart for converting beans to grams and their (re)invention of the principle of scaling. She then went on to add that, as a result of what she was learning about the children from the concerns and capabilities that they manifested, she was gradually changing her way of teaching. Progressively, she realized, she was allowing them a greater share in the responsibility for deciding what tasks they would tackle and how they would approach them; for, as she saw, they became much more fully engaged and more prepared to respond to challenges when the problems they struggled with were ones they had initiated or taken over and made their own.

A second issue that she was thinking about, partly as a result of some collaborative work we had already undertaken (see chapter 3), was certain important similarities that seemed to exist between carrying out an inquiry, such as the work the children were doing on the chicks, and the processes they engaged in when writing. In particular, conferencing with the teacher seemed to serve a very similar function in the two kinds of activity. From these reflections, the topic for her inquiry was gradually taking shape. For both myself and the teacher, this discussion and others like it played an important part in our learning.

However, although the principle of collaborative research under-lay the design of the project from the beginning, we were not, initially, very successful in putting our principles into practice. With hindsight, it is easy to identify the underlying causes of our difficulties in establishing effective collaborative relationships be-tween teachers, administrators, and researchers. First, old habits and attitudes were difficult to overcome, and neither teachers nor researchers had very precise ideas about how to establish a different working relationship from the one that has traditionally held in classroom research. Second, the other declared aim of the project— to carry out a three-year longitudinal study of a particular group of children in whichever classrooms they happened to be placed, and to make comparisons between groups based on quantitative data that were collected according to an overall plan that the teachers, initially, had no part in shaping—seemed to belie our concern to make the research responsive to the questions that the teachers themselves might want to investigate.

Here is how one of the teachers described her initial reaction to the project:

> I became involved in collaborative research and learning by in-heritance, not design. Some of my students had been tracked for two years by the Language and Learning team. My initial reaction was to live with the inclusion of one or two researchers in my classroom. They were as a piece of acetate laid upon an overhead projector, but without the light turned on. Gradually, through discussion and the development of mutual respect and trust, I found the switch. Here were two people who would assist me in investigating three areas of personal concern: co-determination of

curriculum by students and teachers; effective conferencing; and collaboration.

It would be through collaboration that I would obtain answers to my other two concerns—sometimes small insights take a long time to become explicit!

In fact, as this quotation suggests, the breakthrough, when it did come, was not the outcome of a carefully planned change in the design of the project. Rather, it was the cumulative result of a number of small but significant initiatives. The first occurred at the end of the first year when meetings were arranged by grade level for the teachers who had been involved in the project. Each teacher was invited to bring to the meeting some "data" from their classroom that they would like to share with their colleagues. We offered to make video recordings of episodes of interest and several teachers took up this offer. The result was that at these meetings, for the first time, we engaged in very worthwhile discussion, based on evidence of various kinds, of *issues of the teachers' own choosing*.

It was this latter point that was to prove important for the development of collaborative research. For, although none of the teachers involved in this first round continued their participation in the project when the children we were observing moved into the next grades at the beginning of the following year, the meetings had demonstrated to both teachers and researchers that there was much going on in the teachers' classrooms that could serve as the basis for fruitful *joint* inquiry. But, for this to happen, the topics had to arise out of the specifics of the teachers' own classroom practice and to be selected by them in the light of their own concerns.

Having learned this important lesson, we held similar meetings near the beginning and end of each of the remaining two years of the project. In the later rounds, a theme for each meeting was negotiated in advance, which served as a guide for the teachers in selecting the data that they chose to present and provided a focus for the ensuing discussion (Blake, in press). For some of the teachers, these meetings led to the formulation of an inquiry topic that they pursued in collaboration with the school-based researcher over a period of several months (e.g., Shechter and Singleton, in press) and, in one case, led to the formation of a school-based research group that continued to work together after the end of the project, producing booklets for parents and teachers, and an accompanying videotape on the use of across-grade "buddying" in reading and writing (Frankland Inquiry Group 1989).

The second development, although different in its point of departure, also owed its success to the uptake of concerns voiced by the two teachers involved. In both cases, the teachers wished to introduce a new way of working in the classroom and saw the presence of researchers as a resource that could be drawn upon in documenting the effects of the change and, in one case, as an additional support for the children's learning. Both projects led to the making of audio and video recordings of groups of children engaged in tasks that were, from the teachers' points of view, experimental. In each case, the collaborative attempt to interpret the evidence thus collected led to increased understanding of the issues involved on the part of all concerned. And this, in turn, affected the teachers' subsequent practice (see chapter 6).

From these experiences, an understanding was beginning to develop of the conditions that, if not necessary, are at least likely to be facilitative of fruitful collaboration between teachers and researchers in classroom-based inquiry. The first of these conditions has already been mentioned: the importance of the topic selected being one of the teacher's own choosing. As one of the teachers who herself became a teacher-researcher said to the children in her class: "You have to care about your topic." And, in most cases, this means starting with an issue that arises from the teacher's own practice.

Secondly, participation must be voluntary. Although as teacher-educators, we may believe that classroom-based inquiry is likely to be of great benefit to any teacher who undertakes it, the decision to become involved must be the teacher's. Because of the longitudinal design of our project, many teachers became involved — at least initially — simply because of the presence of "target" children in their classrooms. Under these conditions, the invitation to undertake a collaborative inquiry was perceived more coercively than it was intended. However, by the end of the second year, several of the teachers had become sufficiently convinced of the value of collaborative work to ask to continue with the same children for a further year and to carry out a more systematic inquiry.

The third condition that we came to recognize as of overriding importance was time. Time, first, for the participants to get to know each other and to build up the relationship of mutual respect and trust that is essential if they are to be willing to risk having their assumptions challenged by the evidence collected and by another person's interpretation of it (Newman 1987). Time, secondly, for the activities involved in carrying out an inquiry: meetings to plan what has to be done and to discuss the results, suitable occasions for collecting whatever type of data has been decided on, and analysis of these data to generate evidence relevant to the topic under investigation. In the busy schedules of teachers, there is little time to give to these additional tasks, and this inevitably means that progress is slower than one would wish.

Finally, and perhaps most important of all the conditions that need to be met, is a willingness to learn on the part of *all* those involved. In proposing collaborative research as a mode of professional development for teachers, the emphasis naturally tends to fall on what teachers can learn from undertaking an inquiry in their own classroom. However, it is equally important for the researcher to be a learner, too. What each participant learns from the joint undertaking may be different — as is to be expected, given the rather different concerns they bring to the situation — but, without an openness on the part of the researcher as well as the teacher to new understandings about ways in which effective learning opportunities can be created, it is unlikely that a truly collaborative relationship can develop.

As we were considering how we could modify the overall design of the project to come closer to meeting these conditions, an opportunity arose that gave focus to our planning. The annual convention of the International Reading Association was to be held in Toronto in May 1988. What an excellent conclusion to the project it would be, we thought, if we could put together a symposium at the convention in which the outcomes of some of our collaborative research were presented. Four teachers were approached and asked if they would be interested, and all agreed. The principal of one of the schools also asked to be included, and his offer was accepted with enthusiasm. Over the next nine months, the four teachers met with their researcher partners to plan and carry out their respective inquiries, spurred on by the approaching deadline. Then, as the time drew nearer, we began to meet as a group to plan the presentation itself and to work on the texts from which the individual presenters were going to speak.

At this point, we made a further discovery. Although each of the four projects had already reached its conclusion — at least as far as the current cycle of inquiry was concerned — a new sort of learning now began, as each presenter struggled to find an appropriate way of explaining to others what she or he had already come to understand personally. Working under the umbrella title of the symposium, "Improving opportunities for literacy learning through teacher-researcher collaboration," we began to discover just how writing can be a tool for learning and how the conferencing that followed each presenter's first draft could indeed help him or her to discover new meanings in what had been written and to identify points that needed further elaboration or clarification. The preparation of the symposium was thus not simply an occasion for bringing together what had already been learned but, more important, it was, an occasion of literate learning and continuing teacher-researcher collaboration for all those involved.

The Teachers' Voices

The symposium itself took place in a cinema hall adjacent to one of the convention hotels. The audience, although typical in size for a conference event occurring in parallel with many others, was scattered across the two hundred or so available seats, and so seemed smaller and more distant than we would have wished. For many of the speakers, this was their first experience of making a public presentation of this kind. Nevertheless, for all of us it was a memorable occasion. Our collaboration had quite evidently borne fruit. I should like to try to capture the essence of the occasion by quoting from some of the papers that were presented (Chang, et al. 1988).

Branko Deronja: "My assumptions were challenged."

Branko Deronja, who was teaching a combined grade one and two class, decided to investigate "children's problem solving as evidenced in improvisational dramatic play." With the researcher Mei Lian Lam to videotape episodes of dramatic play and interview the children to discover their views on this activity, he wanted to discover how the children would solve the problems that spontaneously arose in the course of their play and how he himself could assist them. When would his intervention be helpful and when would it constitute interference?

> In order to stimulate drama in my room I created a physical space conducive to play. I provided a dress-up box, large blocks for building sets, and various theatrical props. I told the children that they were free to use this space every day after recess. From the beginning, the "Play Corner," as the drama center became known, attracted the same small group of children. The others preferred to spend this time in other interest centers. At first, the children who chose to play there simply delighted in dressing up, sometimes alone and at other times with friends. After a few weeks, children effortlessly stepped into role-playing. Their choice of plots came from three sources: re-enactment of a well-known story, such as Goldilocks or Snow White; a spontaneous idea which came to them through a shared personal experience; or children often chose me as their third source of ideas for plots. They devised variations on the theme that I, the storyteller, featured that particular week.

Children quickly accepted that they could not depend on me to help them with their problems. This was precisely the point of my inquiry. How do children resolve problems on their own in improvisational dramatic play? In order to find answers to this question I kept a log book in which I dutifully noted the nature of the problem and the solution reached.

It was immediately evident that children loved to role-play. They delighted in dressing up, devising plot situations, or simply engaging in what I saw as unfocused random activity. The major benefit at first evident to me was that the players made extraordinary efforts to cooperate with each other. A tantrum, or bossiness, usually isolated that individual. He or she then had to play alone. The pleasure was greater in playing within the group. The first few months made me quite anxious. The play situations or plots did not seem focused; children appeared to play in a random fashion. At this stage, I introduced the rest of the class as their audience. I hoped that this intervention would change the nature of their play—that there would be more planning, greater cohesiveness evident in their play. I had hoped that the children would ultimately come to solutions which would be in harmony with my own criteria for a successful presentable play. In that, I was disappointed.

Branko described what *he* perceived to be the problem: an absence of preplanning and an alarming tendency to change roles on the spur of the moment. This sort of spontaneous improvisation would, in his estimation, inevitably lead to a breakdown of the drama into "exuberant random play" or, still worse, "deteriorate into a discipline problem." But the children proved him wrong. In terms of both the players' and the audience's judgments, the plays were a great success. What is more, their plays showed evidence of effective problem solving—but of the children's problems, not the teacher's.

To demonstrate what he meant, Branko then showed a video recording of an episode from one of his children's plays.

The plot here is derived from our study of Mozart's *Magic Flute*. At this stage, all the children were thoroughly familiar with the story. We also sang many themes from the opera. The music enhanced the story. Children now effortlessly improvised. In the scene recorded on the videotape they chose to dramatize the marriage of the main protagonists. The marriage ceremony is about to be performed by Papageno. But this is not his role. He has, in fact, switched roles and now wants to be a priest. The original and legitimate priest, Sarastro, also wants to perform the marriage ceremony. Here we have a problem caused by role-switching. Which character will stay? The children resolve this conflict on the spot. The legitimate priest, Sarastro, is declared sick. He is rushed to the emergency department of a hospital. The marriage ceremony can now proceed. After the wedding, Papageno announces a pie-eating contest. The rest of the cast is clearly surprised; this is spontaneous and it had not been planned. Papageno takes advantage of the surprise and wins the contest. Random, unfocused, happy dance follows these proceedings, until Papageno, now clearly the leader, announces the end of the play.

This [example] shows that preplanning a play is not essential. In fact, much of the fun, and certainly Papageno's surprise trick, came from the improvisational nature of this play. The conflict caused by Papageno butting in — which would normally create bad feelings — was resolved amicably. When the action became diffuse, the leader made a quick decision. The choice was to allow the random play to continue until a new focus was reached, or to end the play. I am particularly pleased that here we have evidence that children were able to solve their own problems as they encountered them. All had to communicate and co-operate. It was indeed the commitment to co-operation that allowed this play to proceed.

The shift of focus from my concern with their final performance to a concern with the process, and the shift of leadership from me to the children, bore unexpected benefits. My assumptions were challenged.

Helen Whaley: "Making connections among learning, teaching, and research."

Just as Branko Deronja was led to change his assumptions by what he observed, so did Helen Whaley's inquiry lead to revision — not only of her beliefs but also of the execution of the inquiry itself. Her inquiry, entitled "Writing Conferences and the Development of Research Skills," was carried out in collaboration with Gen Ling Chang and Ilda Januario in the context of a unit in which her grade six students researched topics of their own choosing. Her aim was to discover which of three modes of conferencing would be most effective: face-to-face interaction, a carefully written response to the student's work, or a combination of both oral and written modes. To help her to evaluate the effectiveness of each mode, she asked the students to keep written logs, and she herself decided to do the same. However, as she reports, the best laid plans ...!

The problem with my neat little research design soon became apparent as we proceeded. As a teacher, I found I could not carry out my plan to restrict one group to written responses only. What do you, as a teacher, do when a student asks for assistance? Can you say, "Write down your problem and I'll mail back an answer tomorrow"? Or how about when a student says, "I can't read what you wrote" or "What do you mean by this?" Well, so much for written conferences only!

Another problem was the log-keeping. It was not a popular activity, although it contributed to the students becoming more reflective, and sometimes helped them to make their intentions more explicit. Most students avoided writing theirs, and so specific directions from me were required. The students saw it as a waste of time, something that kept them from the pleasure of working on their research topics or conferencing with their peers. In their words, it was a "pain." . . . As for the proposed teacher's log, I, too, soon abandoned it as being too cumbersome. . . . So back to my anecdotal note-keeping—perhaps less organized, but more informative for me in the long run. In my notes, I had a tangible record of a student's progress over time.

My experience has indicated that certain quantitative research designs—such as comparing treatment groups—do not work for the teacher-researcher, because they conflict with teaching. I was constantly revising my original design in order to teach.

Yet, as she goes on to show in her documentation of the research projects the students undertook and what they learned from them, "there are research methods that complement teaching, such as keeping a log, or using audio- or video-tapes and photographs." Her report contains detailed evidence based on each of these methods of data collection and, like her students, she was able to make use of a variety of modes of representation to enliven her presentation.

Choosing an appropriate form for the information to be conveyed and for the audience to be addressed, in fact, turned out to be an important occasion of learning for all concerned.

In our conferencing, both formal and informal, we encouraged the students to consider various modes of representing the knowledge they were gaining. An information booklet might not be the only form, especially if one intended to convey information to various audiences in interesting ways. The students were challenged to consider the kinds of knowledge they were going to include, to be aware that different kinds of knowledge required or were enhanced by different forms of expression, and to consider the use of technology, models, demonstrations, charts, etc., to further illuminate their subject. The joint exploration between students and adults about how they would represent and communicate the specialized knowledge gained, was an engagement in the literate process of thinking about the nature of textual forms.

Their awareness of audience, and the role audience played in their composition of various text types, increased as peers came to inquire, offer assistance or give an opinion on ongoing work.

[At this point slides were shown to show conferencing of various kinds and at various stages in the students' research.]

With interest expressed by class members, it was decided to share our knowledge with other classes, rather than just among ourselves. This contrasted again with their previous research experience and made for a different type of audience — an audience who had not shared in the research experiences and so did not have insiders' assumptions. The promise of a real audience led individual students towards considering more interactive modes of presentation. When the audience came, the students became acutely aware of audience behaviour and whether they could capture the audience's interests — either by their initial display or by their role as experts. . . .

Personality played a key role. Wei-Ming reached out and captured an audience every time, regardless of age, and the discussion was animated and interesting. Others, like Eddie, looked for ways of attracting an audience so he could share his knowledge about China. On the first day he brought real money. Surprisingly, that was not enough; so, on the second, he revised his strategy and added samples of Chinese food and made Jasmine tea.

Throughout our work, the audience factor pushed all of us, students and adults alike, to search for greater clarity of thought and action. In our collaboration with each other, we discussed the pros and cons of the various text forms we entertained, and considered the effectiveness each had on different types of audiences.

If the highest form of literate behaviour is the production of external representations of what we have come to know, then these students have become more literate, more aware, and more versatile in their literacy.

On conferencing — the initial subject of her inquiry — Helen concluded that "the written and oral modes each had their contribution." However, as she suggested at the outset, this was eventually less important to her than some of the other things she learned as a result of engaging in a systematic, collaborative inquiry. One of these, made possible by the presence of other adults to share the conferencing with students, was the value of having "time to really see the learning styles and needs of each student, and to respond to them." It is the value of collaboration itself though, that she emphasizes in her conclusion.

For me, the power of teacher-researcher collaboration in the classroom is the ability of different communities to share their knowledge, to have their concepts challenged or confirmed, while making connections among learning, teaching, and research. The connections were at two levels: children and adults, and teacher and researchers.

From my experience, all three constellations—the learner, the teacher-researcher, and the researchers—shared each other's roles and benefited from the amalgam.

Ann Maher: *"My professional behavior in the classroom has changed."*

Ann Maher is the teacher in whose classroom the observation that opened this chapter was made. As was mentioned earlier, she started with an interest in the relationship between writing and inquiry more generally and, by the time she started the inquiry reported here, she had sharpened her question considerably. The context was a unit of study on living creatures (see chapter 5) and her question was phrased as follows: "If I familiarize my Grade Four students with the language of revision, will there be an observable difference in their daily writing? An additional and perhaps equally important question has been Does my involvement in collaborative research change my behavior in the classroom?"

In her presentation, Ann spoke about the way in which, over the course of the year, what had started as a relatively limited inquiry became more and more pervasive in her thinking about learning and teaching.

> As my students worked, I noticed that some were formulating inappropriate questions: too difficult, too simple, or even some that were impossible to answer. A student asked if she could change her topic. Although I responded positively to the child's request, the necessity of allowing and encouraging this step had never occurred to me before. I now realized I had to treat the sign-up sheet as a first draft. . . .
>
> In discussions with colleagues on the research team, I realized that I had to revise my ideas about revision. Until now, I had been so concerned with my failure to nudge kids into revising more than a word here and there in their written ideas that I had not taken the time to step back from the problem to think deeply about the nature and process of revision itself. I am beginning to see that revision is a much broader concept. It has everything to do with reflecting on ideas and plans and making changes where it seems most reasonable to do so. I was to learn much in the days that followed about how my hazy notions had prevented my students as well as myself from a clearer understanding.

Later in her talk, Ann went on to describe a "critical incident," quoting Newman (1987), which brought this point home to her with particular force. As she ruefully recognized, the incident was particularly ironic in the light of her chosen topic. Commenting on an episode she had just shown on videotape, in which groups reviewed a list of types of learning that they had generated before the project started (see transcript p. 116), she writes:

> Watching this tape, I marvelled at their intense efforts to articulate their ideas precisely. But I was startled to discover that I had managed to introduce this revision task without once using the word "revision." Chagrined, I had to admit that, in the classroom, I avoided the word at all costs. Like the children, I use the language that I am familiar and comfortable with. My uncertainty and confusion are inherent in my behaviour.

> Hence it came as no surprise that none of my students interviewed by Mei Lian [the researcher] could define the term "revision." Some students had some notion of the process but they were not familiar with the word and confused it with editing. But the day after, I began to consciously use more explicit language — to put the label on the action called revision. The children interviewed began to imitate my language and were able to define revision more satisfactorily.

> I had intended to speak [today] about how I used the term "revision" extensively to introduce the writing process in the fall, for I believed that "revision" was prominent in my writing charts, available, I thought proudly, as a valuable aid to my students. Mei Lian and I talked about using the chart as concrete evidence. Considering this possibility I turned to examine the chart.

> I had done it again. The word "revision" was conspicuous by its absence. I am not suggesting that my error of omission is of such monumental importance in itself. Although the children may not know the term "revision," they do engage in revision behaviour — which is much more important. Yet, the significance lies in my lack of awareness. It is the teacher's daily practices and the message inherent in that behaviour that affects our students. You may be interested to know that my students helped to revise this chart — they decided where revision belonged in the total process.

> One change is related to another. As I become a more reflective practitioner, in turn my changing behavior seems to have a more immediate effect on the children. I am constantly reminded that what the teacher demonstrates with sincerity has the greatest impact. Being thoroughly involved with revision not only intellectually but also physically in the writing and revising of this paper, I told my class about my project. Intrigued, they wanted to know more. I showed them my paper, full of cut and paste, reworkings, and addenda. To encourage their involvement in the process, I suggested that they might look through their folders for a piece of writing that they might like to revise. Marie rewarded me with a rewrite of an October story that had been crude and needlessly violent to a more subtle and powerful piece.

In formulating for us her recognition of the crucial role of revision, not only in writing, but in all forms of purposeful activity, Ann made explicit a principle that is at the heart of our growing understanding of the value of action research undertaken as a form of professional development: Change in practice that leads to improved learning opportunities for students is most likely to occur when it is conceived as revision, that is to say when it starts by the practitioner carefully observing her or his current ways of working, and then "reflecting on ideas and plans and making changes where it seems most reasonable to do so."

In concluding her presentation, Ann returned to this theme by reconsidering her second question: "Does my involvement in collaborative research change my behavior in the classroom?" This is the answer she gave: "Although my inquiry is far from complete, my professional behaviour in the classroom has changed, as the children and I are drawn more closely together into a community of learners working to explore, to reflect, and, in the light of new information, to revise old assumptions and to expand our understanding of the processes of thinking and learning."

The Administrator's Voice

It was this powerful effect on their practice that Dietrich Golanska had noticed as he visited the classrooms of the teachers in his school who had become involved in collaborative research. And it was the potential of this form of professional development activity for bringing about educational change that had led him to join the symposium panel. Inspired by what he had seen, his hope was now to make teacher research a central part of his school policy for teacher development and evaluation.

However, he started by explaining how he, too, had had his original assumptions challenged by his experiences during the course of the project. Like the teachers who had talked about the importance of giving students more responsibility for choosing their own topics and the ways in which they would investigate and present them, he too had had to learn that educational leadership is less a matter of exercising control and more one of encouraging and supporting the learning initiatives of others and providing an environment in which they feel able to take risks and to share their ideas — their doubts and disappointments as well as their successes — with colleagues who are equally committed to learning through collaborative inquiry. He stated, "Today, the teachers who spoke to you are good examples of our enterprise. They are educators who, through collaborative research in their classrooms, have been able to examine, explicate, and reflect on their own practices. The greater understanding they have gained has opened up possibilities and opportunities within the area of teacher development that, in my opinion, have previously not existed."

Then, having described some of the particular activities that had taken place in the school during the course of the project, he summarized his view of the value of teacher-researcher collaboration, and spoke about his hopes for the future:

> From my position as principal, I felt that there were three positive aspects to this project:
>
> 1. Researcher and teacher became partners who were jointly concerned with the classroom life of the children, and especially with the provision of learning opportunities.
> 2. The teacher, through systematic study about her or his own topic of inquiry, developed a personal theory of applicability of curricular decision making.
> 3. The teachers changed their notions about professional development. Being active and self-determining participants in their own growth made them realize that they became agents of change, and not just patients.
>
> ... Last, but not least, is our recent formation of an inquiry group, made up of the school librarian, five teachers from across the grades, myself, two ward consultants (language and science), and three researchers from the Language and Learning Project. Several members of this group are already tied closely to some research exercises. This collaborative structure is our attempt to shift thinking about "my classroom" in isolation to thinking, with others, about "my classroom" within the larger institutional context of the school. It is also my hope that such a group of emerging in-house teachers-as-researchers will in time conduct professional development, curriculum planning and development, so that these educational concerns could in very real ways be a joint enterprise within our staff.

The School as a Center of Inquiry

In these closing words, Dietrich Golanska spoke to the ultimate aim of our project, to give practical expression to a vision of "the school as a center of inquiry," in which the values of caring, collaboration, and curiosity would be manifested in the creation of "communities of literate thinkers" not only in each classroom, but also in the staff room, in the local teachers' center, and also in the board of education's central office. His action, as principal of the school, in setting up an inquiry group that included members from outside the school as well as those teachers on the staff who were interested in participating, was a bold attempt to create an administrative structure within which this vision could become a reality.

Sadly, the inquiry group did not long outlive the ending of the project. The school became involved in a major administrative reorganization, there were changes in staff, including the promotion of one of the teacher-researchers to the role of district consultant and, perhaps most important, the request for additional resources to allow participating teachers and one of the researchers to be enabled to take part in meetings of the group was turned down by the central administration because of a lack of funds. In the face of all these setbacks, not surprisingly, the initiative was finally abandoned.

The concept of the school as a center of inquiry is not a new idea. It was first outlined by Schaefer, as long ago as 1967. However, as Schaefer realized then, for this vision to become a reality, there need to be many changes, not only in the attitudes of teachers, but also in the administrative structures within which they work, and in the conceptions of education held by parents, school governers, and those who administer the public funds collected through national and local taxation. There is clearly still a long way to go.

Nevertheless, the contribution of the Language and Learning Project to the achievement of this goal was not entirely insignificant. In the first place, the lives and learning opportunities of Marilda, João, Salvatore, and many other children were enriched by the experiences that, as a result of their willingness to explore new possibilities, their teachers created for and with them. This, in itself, is a worthwhile achievement. Indeed, it is the ultimate goal of all attempts to bring about educational change. The teachers, too, were significantly changed by the experience, as their own words eloquently testify. The effects of the project were also felt more widely, as key persons in other jurisdictions, who attended the symposium described above, were inspired to explore what might be achieved along similar lines in their own spheres of work.[5]

But perhaps most important, in the present context, is the effect that participation in the project had on the authors of the papers collected in this book. For me, the opportunity to work collaboratively on classroom inquiries with a group of committed and resourceful teachers was a new and rewarding experience. I owe much to the insights gained in our joint exploration of the topics they chose to investigate and of the evidence that we collected. It was through talking with them and with my colleagues in the research team, and through the writing and reading that went on in parallel, that I came to my present understanding of the centrality of literate thinking as both the goal and means of education. For it is through engagement with written texts and other symbolic artifacts, and through the talk with others that surrounds and complements our more solitary reading and writing, that we most effectively address the problems that concern us and contribute to the well-being of the other members of the communities to which we belong.

Notes

Chapter One

1. Interestingly, as we discovered from our interviews with the children and their parents, while parents and other adults in the home most frequently conversed with the children in the first language of the parents, the children most frequently used English when conversing with their siblings and peers.

2. The results of this longitudinal study can be found in the first three volumes of the final report, *Language and Learning: Learners, Teachers and Researchers at Work*, which is being published by the Ontario Ministry of Education.

3. The story of this project is told in *The meaning makers: Children learning language and using language to learn*. Gordon Wells. Portsmouth, NH: Heinemann, 1986.

4. This is, in fact, the strategy that has been adopted by the National Oracy Project in Britain, as teachers have explored their own ways of achieving the objectives laid down by the National Curriculum Council (Norman, 1992).

5. One such outcome was the adoption of classroom inquiry as the main mode of teachers' professional development in the Peel Project, "Talk: A Medium for Learning and Change" (Booth and Thornley-Hall, 1991), in which both the authors of this volume were subsequently involved.

Chapter Two

Talk for Learning and Teaching

Given the pervasiveness of talk in classrooms, at all levels of education, it is surprising to find how little detailed attention it has received, either from researchers or from educational theorists. Little is known, for instance, about the types of tasks that are most likely to promote talk in which students make new and productive connections between their own ideas and those of others, nor about the types of teacher intervention that foster rather than interrupt — or, worse still, suppress — such thoughtful talk. With the exception of the work of a small number of teachers and teacher-educators, which is largely associated, in the English-speaking countries, with the professional organizations for the teaching of English, most writers on learning and teaching, both generally and in relation to specific curricular subjects, have tended to treat talk as straightforward and unproblematic. Like a window, it appears to them to be transparent, allowing them to look through it to focus on the "real" issues of teaching and learning.

My aim in this chapter will be to try to correct this misconception by offering a theoretical perspective from which talk is seen to be the very essence of educational activity. I shall then explore two courses of action that may lead it to be given its rightful place in thinking about classroom practice. First, however, I wish to suggest an explanation for the disregard it has suffered in the past.

The Emphasis on the Individual

Since the inception of publicly provided universal education, debate about both goals and means has been dominated by two competing

26

ideologies. The first and, without doubt, the strongest of these ideologies conceives of schooling as a form of socialization, by means of which successive generations are trained to maintain the existing intellectual and social order (Apple 1990). In this tradition, the emphasis is placed on the imparting of culturally valued knowledge and skills (Hirsch 1987), which are delivered according to a predetermined schedule designed by experts outside the classroom. Under such a conception, the dominant mode in which the teaching-learning relationship is realized is inevitably one of transmission and reception: the curriculum is presented through teacher exposition and approved texts, and students are expected to learn through attentive listening and reading and through solitary study, with an emphasis on comprehending rather than questioning the information presented. Student writing, although valued in theory, is in practice used mainly as a medium for evaluating mastery and retention of what has been taught (Britton et al. 1975), while speaking is tolerated only under strict teacher control and almost exclusively in the response role of answering display questions designed to check comprehension and maintain attention (Hammersley 1977; Heap 1985).

In opposition to this ideology of cultural reproduction, there have been repeated, but largely unsuccessful, attempts to place the learner at the center of the educational enterprise. Dubbed "progressive" in contrast to the prevailing "traditional" pedagogy, this ideology has emphasized creativity as opposed to conformity, and active exploration as opposed to passive reception, in the students' encounters with the curriculum (Dewey 1900; Plowden 1967). In recent years, drawing support from the findings of Piaget's research into genetic epistemology, proponents of this ideology have achieved considerable success, particularly in the elementary years, in placing the emphasis on learning through discovery and in making instruction dependent on students' "readiness" which, it is believed, is largely a function of individual, biologically-determined maturation. Whereas in the traditional classroom, the teacher is the dispenser and arbiter of knowledge, in the progressive classroom it is the individual child's active construction of knowledge that is the organizing principle, with the teacher's role being that of stage-managing experiences to support the students' largely autonomous learning. However, even in this classroom, although there is much more talk as students engage in a variety of practical activities, it is not accorded a primary role since, according to the interpretation put upon Piaget's work, talk serves only for the expression of thought and not as the medium in which thought is shaped and developed.

However, although these two ideologies are in stark opposition with respect to the underlying conceptions of the nature of learning — and hence of the role of the teacher — they have tended in the actual practice of the majority of teachers to coexist in an uneasy compromise. Even in the most traditional classrooms, teachers make provision for some hands-on experiential learning and include class discussion as part of the repertoire of activities, though in both cases keeping firm control over the knowledge that is constructed in the process. And, as Edwards and Mercer (1987) so powerfully demonstrate, teachers who subscribe to the progressive ideology feel an equally strong obligation to ensure that what their students learn from their active explorations is in conformity with the knowledge that is enshrined in the curriculum. In neither case, therefore, do students typically have the opportunity to make their *own* sense of the learning opportunities that are presented to them and to do so *in collaborative interaction* with their peers and with others more knowledgeable than themselves. Not surprisingly, therefore, since collaborative sense-making is not a primary objective under either ideology, little attention has been given to the talk in which such co-construction of meaning might occur.

The reason for this, I suggest, is to be found in what these two ideologies have in common, namely, an essentially individualistic conception of learning. For whether conceived of as an empty vessel waiting to be filled, or as a plant that needs to be nurtured to enable it to achieve its full potential, the learner is seen in either case as independent and self-contained, and learning activities as taking place *within* individuals rather than in transactions *between* them. Furthermore, because knowledge — whether learner-constructed or teacher-transmitted — is taken in both ideologies to be an individual possession, with language serving only to communicate what is known, little attention is given to the task-related discourse in which knowledge is collaboratively constructed, validated, and modified in the purposeful activities in which learners engage with others in the cultural communities of home or school.[6]

Learning and Teaching as Social Transaction

There is, however, a well-developed alternative to these individualistic theories of learning in the sociocultural theory pioneered by Vygotsky and extended by his colleagues and followers (Vygotsky 1962, 1978, 1981; Forman et al., in press; Moll 1990; Newman et al. 1989; Rogoff 1990; Rogoff and Lave 1984; Wertsch 1985a, 1985b).

Central to the work of this school of thought is the recognition of the interdependence of individual and society, as each creates and is created by the other. Although on different time scales, both are the outcome of the innumerable occasions of purposeful interpersonal interaction that make up everyday life. With respect to society, as Vygotsky makes clear, "culture is the product of social life and of human social activity" (1981, p. 168). But the obverse is equally important: individual activity is always specific to a particular culture at a particular point in the historical development of that culture and dependent on the tools that the culture makes available. Thus, like the culture itself, the individual's knowledge, and the repertoire of actions and operations by means of which he or she carries out the activities that fulfill his or her perceived needs, are both constructed in the course of solving the problems that arise in goal-directed social activity and learned through interpersonal interaction. Human development and learning are thus intrinsically social and interactive.

In recent work by Rogoff and her colleagues (e.g., Rogoff 1990), this concept of cultural learning has been explored in terms of the metaphor of "apprenticeship". Following Vygotsky (1978), she sees learning as occurring through the participation of a "novice" in a jointly undertaken cultural activity, in which the "expert" assists the novice's performance and, through demonstration, guidance, and explanation, enables her to appropriate and internalize the cultural ways of carrying out the activity. On any occasion, the learner is given responsibility for those parts of the task that she can already perform and is helped with those that she cannot yet manage alone, with the expert ensuring that the task as a whole is brought to a satisfactory completion. In this way, learning is always undertaken in the context of a meaningful activity, with the significance of the component parts being understood in relation to the achievement of the goal of the activity as a whole; furthermore, the aim is that the learner should ultimately be able to carry out the complete task on her own.

To be maximally effective, the guidance and assistance that the adult gives in such joint problem-solving situations needs to be responsive to the learner's own intentions and understanding, and pitched slightly beyond her current level of unaided performance. This band between what the learner can already manage alone and the upper limit of what she can do with help is what Vygotsky called the "zone of proximal development." It is in this zone that teaching should occur. "Instruction is good," he wrote, "only when it proceeds ahead of development; [then it] awakens and rouses to life an entire set of functions which are in the stage of maturing, which lie in the zone of proximal development" (1934, p. 222, quoted in Wertsch 1985b, p. 71).

Summed up in Vygotsky's aphorism, "What the child can do today with help, tomorrow he will be able to do alone," the concept of learning through apprenticeship is already familiar with respect to such practical activities as children learning to feed and dress themselves. At first, the parent has to perform the whole activity — spooning the food into the child's mouth or putting the child's limbs into the arms and legs of the garments. But before very long children attempt to perform some of these actions for themselves, with the parent performing the more difficult parts, such as cutting up the meat or buttoning a shirt, and generally monitoring the activity as a whole to ensure that it is brought to a satisfactory completion. Finally, the child reaches the stage of being able to carry out the whole task unaided.

However, it was actually in relation to the development of the "higher" mental processes, such as deliberate remembering and reasoning, that Vygotsky developed his theory of learning through assisted performance in the context of joint activity (1981). For, just as much as in the case of the practical actions already referred to, Vygotsky considered the development of cognition to result from participation with others in goal-directed activity, in the course of which the learner encounters particular problems and comes to understand and be able to resolve them with the aid of the intellectual tools inherited from previous generations and with the assistance provided by the members of his or her immediate community.

Speech is the first, and probably the most versatile, of these intellectual tools that the culture makes available to the child, enabling him or her to engage in joint thinking with others through the talk that accompanies, directs, and reflects on the problem solving required in everyday social activity (Halliday 1975). This external, social, speech is then gradually internalized to become a resource that can be used by the child, when alone, for individual thinking and problem solving in the mode that Vygotsky called "inner speech." In this way, the development of the higher mental functions starts as *inter*mental, social behavior and becomes appropriated and transformed into *intra*mental, individual behavior. The higher mental functions are thus, as Wertsch (1981) puts it, "the mediated internalized result of social interaction" (p. 147).

A similar process takes place in learning to use the semiotic tool provided by the written mode of language use. As recent research has shown (Hall 1987), learners are best able to appropriate the skills necessary to participate in the cultural practices of literacy when they are involved in joint literacy events in which the form and function of written texts is demonstrated in the context of a meaningful activity. However, because reading and writing are essentially mental activities — and therefore unobservable — it is crucial that the adult not only assist the learner to participate in the task, but that he or she also engage with the learner in talk about the text that externalizes in speech the internal mental processes involved in reading or writing (see chapter 7). This engagement will involve discussion of the content of the text and its significance for the activity in which it is being used, and also metalinguistic talk about the strategies that a reader or writer uses in engaging with a text to achieve his or her purpose on that occasion (Palincsar and Brown 1984). Like learning to talk, becoming literate is thus a cultural apprenticeship involving social interaction with other readers and writers, as well as an individual cognitive achievement. Indeed, as Rogoff (1990) puts it, individual literacy would not be possible without "models provided by other people who read and assist in learning to read, or without a literate society in which there is material and reason to read and a system to organize written communication" (p. 26).

But it is in relation to the learning of what Vygotsky calls schooled or "scientific" concepts — that is, the organized ways of thinking that are appropriate to the different subject disciplines encountered in formal education — that talk assumes the greatest importance as the mediator of higher mental functions and in the appropriation and internal reconstruction of cultural knowledge. For cultural knowledge of this kind is essentially discursive in nature. It is constructed in the dialogue, both spoken and written, through which practitioners maintain, modify, and develop the theories and interpretive practices that constitute the different disciplines. Thus, to be a physicist or a historian *is* to participate in the discourse of physics or history, and to learn those subjects is to undertake an apprenticeship into the modes of discourse through which the relevant cultural meanings are sustained and developed.

The metaphor of apprenticeship has certainly illuminated our understanding of the way in which cultural practices are enacted and appropriated in the context of joint activities. However, we should be careful to remember the goal of this form of learning, which is that learners should be able to make use of the knowledge and skills they have appropriated from the culture to contribute to the solution of *new* problems in ways that go *beyond* what they have inherited. Unless this is kept in mind, and encouragement given to learners' own constructive efforts and to the novel solutions to problems that they propose, there is a danger that the theory of learning as "assisted performance" will be used to further bolster the traditional practices of transmission-based instruction, rather than providing the basis for a radical and empowering alternative. In work carried out to date from the sociocultural perspective (e.g., Newman et al. 1989), the emphasis has indeed tended to be placed on the means whereby learners appropriate the cultural heritage through guided participation in collaborative activity. The challenge is now to describe and explain how such activities can also enable them to create new ideas and, thereby, to contribute to the transformation and enrichment of that heritage.

Education as Dialogue

So far in this chapter, I have tried to show that when one adopts a sociocultural — as opposed to an individualistic — perspective on education, talk, far from being an unimportant accompaniment to the real business of learning and teaching, is seen to be a central and constitutive part of every activity. In a very important sense, education *is* dialogue.

From the learner's point of view, it is through participation in interaction in the context of joint problem solving with adults that they encounter the meaning-making resources of their culture and stretch their understanding to find common ground with their more skilled and knowledgeable interlocutors (Wells 1990); and, in a complementary way, when they engage in collaborative tasks with peers, they are challenged to construct novel solutions, to consider the alternatives proposed by others, and to justify and clarify their own point of view in order to communicate and to convince (Rogoff 1990; see also chapter 3 in this volume). Then, from having engaged in these activities in the mode of social interaction, they are able to appropriate the dialogic forms of conversation so that they become a resource for thinking in the internal dialogue of inner speech and in the construction of extended spoken and written monologue (Wertsch and Toma 1990).

From the teacher's point of view, the talk that occurs in those same problem-solving activities provides the opportunity to discover the interests and current state of understanding of individual students. Armed with this information, the teacher is then able to select tasks that will provide enticing and challenging learning opportunities and to offer guidance and assistance that is appropriately pitched within the students' zones of proximal development. It is also in this talk that the teacher is able to introduce and demonstrate the relevant cultural tools, that is, the appropriate forms and functions of discourse, in such a way that the teaching is contingently responsive to the students' own efforts to make sense of the topic under investigation.

In sum, it is in the talk through which tasks are defined, negotiated, and evaluated, and by means of which the students' participation is monitored and assisted, that students and teachers engage in the dialogic co-construction of meaning, which is the essence of education.

However, it is one thing to provide a theoretical rationale for the importance of talk in the process of schooling, and quite another to know how to act in conformity with this rationale in all the varied situations that occur in the course of a typical day, week, or term in any particular classroom. This requires a knowledge of the different types of talk that are most appropriate for different purposes and an understanding of the contextual conditions, both enabling and constraining, that influence the effectiveness of the talk for achieving these purposes. At the present moment we are very far from having this sort of knowledge or understanding. Nevertheless, it seems to me that there are two directions we might profitably take in trying to improve on this situation.

The first of these involves what might be called theory-oriented research, based on the close analysis of particular episodes of classroom talk. The aim of such research is to gain a greater understanding of the way in which knowledge is co-constructed over the course of conversation through the sequential contributions of the various participants as they shape their utterances to fit the demands of the situation according to their interpretation of it. From the study of such episodes, selected in a systematic manner, it may be possible to arrive at principles of interaction that have quite general applicability and, in this way, to throw more light on the question of how we learn through talk.

The second direction involves a different, but complementary, form of research, conducted by teachers in their own classrooms as they attempt to improve the learning opportunities they provide for their students, and to gain a firmer basis, through reflection on their own practice, for the moment-by-moment pedagogical decisions that they are called upon to make in the course of every lesson.

So What's Happening?
Making Sense of a Science Activity

To provide a partial illustration of the first line of research, I should like to examine the transcript of an episode of talk that occurred in a unit of study on light in a class of nine- and ten-year-olds.[7] The teacher has arranged a number of exploratory activities, each with problems to be addressed and some guiding instructions on how to approach them, and the students are working in groups, spending some time on each activity in turn. The group in the extract to be examined consists of two girls, Wendy and Rachel (Anglo- and Portuguese-Canadian, respectively), and two boys, Gurmit and Balkrishan (both from the Indian subcontinent). They are working on the topic of refraction and, at the beginning of the extract, have spent some time together exploring the materials and experimenting with the effects of placing a wooden ruler and other similar objects in a glass tank full of water. They have observed that the objects appear to bend as they enter the water.

During the last few minutes, the teacher has joined the group and has been listening to their discussion. At turn 17, the teacher decides to intervene by asking a very general question.

17 T: OK so what's happening?

18 W&R: Bending

19 T: Everything's bending . .

20 G: And refracting

21 T: Well what is "refracting" do you think then?
If you say everything's bending .

22 R: bending

23 T: refracting is — ?

24 R: Bending

25 T: It's bending . OK

The teacher's question could be answered in a variety of ways. However, the students are clearly orienting to the task as it was defined in the printed instructions, since several of them respond in terms of the feature of interest. "Bending" is what they report to be happening. In accepting this formulation, the teacher makes a significant addition. Generalizing their observation with "everything," he implicitly presents it as a phenomenon of scientific interest that calls for an explanation. With this prompt, Gurmit offers an alternative description of what has been observed, using the technical term "refracting". The teacher picks up on this and asks for a verbal definition of refracting, using the description they have already provided as a prelude to his cued elicitation: "Refraction is . . .?" to which the students provide the conversationally appropriate completion: "bending."

At this point, by following the lead offered by Gurmit (in turn 20), a relationship of equivalence has been established by teacher and students together between refraction and bending. However, from a scientific point of view, this is an inadequate definition, since not all instances of bending can be described as refraction. The teacher's pause before adding "OK" in accepting the students' response (25) suggests that he is aware of this, but, rather than implicitly reject their response by providing a more adequate definition of his own, he decides first to find out what sense they have made of the "first little problem" that the activity card had posed for them.

25 T: Now . let's come back to the first little problem you had .. and this is this problem
[T kneels down at the table and indicates a coin in a shallow dish of water. The children gather around T .]

26 R: It's refracting

27 T: Now . let's — OK

28 G: No that isn't refracting

29 T: Something — . just sit down Gurmit OK? (to G)

30 R: Yes 'cos you could see it (pointing to the coin in the dish)
[B and G are now sitting on T's left, W and R are on his right, W standing and R sitting]

31 T: Something had to . happen that had something to do with refraction .. right? (looking at B)

32 B: Yeah

33 W: It reflects

34 R: Yeah it reflects

35 T: What is "reflection"?

36 W: When um — when you put something um in water and then it reflects (making up and down movements with right hand)

37 B: No when you look in the mirror . you're like um reflecting

38 G: Your reflection

39 B: Reflecting is like when — when your image bounces off something and you can see it

40 T: OK . that's reflection right — you look in a mirror . and you see your pretty face .. (looking at R and smiling) Now . is that what we're doing here? Are we seeing something REFLECT? Are we seeing .

41 G: No (shaking his head)

42 T: (looking at R and W) something bounce right back at us the way we were looking at it?

43 G: No

44 W: I can see it right now

45 G: No

46 R: I can see it bending (pointing to dish)

47 G: Yeah but it's not the same it's not exactly how the same . like if we took it out . not . and we put it back in (making taking-and-replacing gestures) and it won't be the same
[R shakes her head in agreement]

48 T: It's . (looking at G, appealing for completion)

49 G: Refracting? (seeking confirmation)
[T smiles questioningly] . reflecting?

50 T: OK . you — you're right . they — they're changed a little
Now . it's not so much that the penny actually changes but . it's that the penny . doesn't seem to be where it really is

51 G: Yeah

52 T: It's not — (looking at ruler in tank) the ruler doesn't really bend . does it?

53 R: Bend

54 W: No

55 G: No

56 T: But it certainly . LOOKS — (seeking completion)

57 W: Bigger
[R pushes the ruler in and out of the tank.]

58 T: Well it does that — but it LOOKS like it's bent doesn't it?

59 All: Yeah (W bends down to check)

60 T: OK? . Now . so refraction has something to do with things that appear to — (seeking completion) . . BEND

61 G: Yeah

62 T: OK now . "reflection" . and . "refraction" . are they the same two things?

63 W&G: No

64 T: No OK that's one point to make sure of
Now . they're — they're totally different . .
[T takes ruler from R and lays it on top of tank]
No just leave it now (to R) . . .
So refraction has something to do with light that . bends

The introduction of "reflection" at 33–34 is certainly part of a complete account of the phenomenon that the teacher is asking the group to consider when he asks them to think about the "first little problem" of the penny in the dish. However, since he has just couched the problem in terms of "something to do with refraction" (31), mention of "reflection" is not discursively relevant at this point and may therefore signal a confusion between the two concepts on the part of the two girls, who offered this contribution. Over the following few exchanges, therefore, the teacher leads the group to see the two concepts as contrastive: reflection is when light is able to "bounce right back at us the way we were looking at it" (42), whereas refraction "has something to do with light that bends" (64).

Having dealt with this potential confusion, the teacher returns to the original task: the construction of an explanation for the phenomenon of the reappearing penny. However — perhaps because he is anxious not to impose his agenda at the expense of ideas that the students might contribute — he first invites those students who have "done the reseach on eyes" to tell what they can about "what is really happening with the light and your eyes" (68).

64 T: Well when you looked first of all . at this — (puts finger on penny to hold it and pours away water in dish) . .
Let's come back to how we actually see it —
Have you people done . the research on eyes yet? (looking at B and G)

65 All: Yeah

66 T: So now you know everything about seeing (looking around group)

67 Ss: Yes

68 T: Tell me how it is you see that penny right now (looking at B and G)
What is really happening with the light and your eyes?

69 G: You're looking —

70 B: The — the light bounces sort of off your eyes . and it hits something like a mirror or something . and then um —
[G picks up his notebook]

71 W: Is this — is this a camera * —
[W goes to get a stool and sits on T's right]

72 B: and then you can see that and . . um —

73 G: It's a pinhole camera . your eye's sort of like a camera
. but really . er we've been looking —

74 R: ** ⟨to the fact that⟩ your brain's —

75 G: Yeah that's what we done . We looked in — in an encyclopedia
Your brain works so fast like if you open your eye . the moment you look at it . your brain ch — turns it right . like you look in the pinhole camera .

76 T: Uh-huh

77 G: We saw something upside down . I don't know why . like we didn't
*** . . your brain didn't fix it

78 T: OK

79 G: So when you look at something . it's upside down but your brain fixes it

80 T: OK we'll come back to that in a minute (softly to G)

81 B: I know . . whe — when we did the pinhole camera um . we got the image upside down like we normally do and then our brain corrected it . but um . it's like .. when the—when we look— ...Oh I dunno (trails away) ..

82 T: Ok that one—that one does .. get a little confusing when you look at the pinhole .
Let's forget the pinhole for a minute we'll—we'll explain that later . but let's look at this one first of all

As Balkrishan takes up the teacher's invitation to tell what they have learned from their research on eyes, it is interesting to note how he formulates his account in the terms that had been used earlier in the jointly constructed account of reflection (39—42): "the light bounces sort of off your eyes . and it hits something like a mirror" (70). However, in this current version, the ambiguity as to the directionality of the movement of light between the reflecting surface and the eyes—an ambiguity that had been inherent in the original formulation—is resolved in a form that the speaker appears to recognize as problematic, for he hesitates and leaves his account incomplete: "you can see that and .. um—" (72).

Meanwhile, Gurmit has made a different connection between the teacher's question and what he has discovered from the research that he and his friend have conducted with the aid of the encyclopedia. It seems that they have been reading about the way in which the brain deals with the inverted image that falls on the retina, with the inversion being explained by reference to what can be observed to occur in the case of the image projected on the back surface of a pinhole camera. In 73, he tentatively tries out this connection by picking up Wendy's reference to "a camera" (71), and when Balkrishan abandons his attempted explanation, Gurmit takes over the floor and develops an alternative explanation—with Balkrishan joining in—in terms of the brain's "fixing" of the inverted image (75—81). However, this attempt also eventually peters out as the two boys find they are unable to make the necessary connection. At this point, the teacher decides to refocus the discussion, while at the same time saving face for all participants by recognizing that it "does .. get a little confusing when you look at the pinhole" (82).

Picking up what is most relevant in the preceding utterances, the teacher now returns to the issue of constructing an explanation for the observation that pouring water into the dish makes it possible for the penny, which had not been visible from their position some distance from the dish, to become once more visible. This is done by taking them through the steps of the demonstration while simultaneously engaging them in talk about the significance of what they observe.

82 **T**: Like you're saying that we see that we see that penny . you said because light comes from somewhere .

83 **G**: Mm

84 **T**: and . it hits the penny .

85 **G**: and bounces off <u>your</u> eye

86 **T**: <u>and</u> . .
that's why <u>we</u> can all see it . right?

87 **W**: <u>Yeah</u>

88 **All**: Yeah (nodding)

89 **T**: Now . when I ask you to back up . . OK do that . back up . . so that you can't see the penny . .
[Children move backwards away from the dish]
Is the light . still hitting the penny?

90 **G**: Yes (W nods)

91 **T**: And is it still bouncing off?

92 **W&G**: Yes

93 **R**: No

94 **T**: Is it not? (to R)

95 **G**: It's bouncing off but—

96 **B**: I think <u>*</u>

97 **T**: <u>All</u> right . you can't see it because it's not hitting your eyes . I can see it . it's bouncing off and it's hitting MY eyes . but for some reason it's not hitting YOUR eyes
So then the light's coming down (gesturing down to penny) . it's hitting here . and . it seems that any of the light that bounces off this penny . and it tries to come towards you (making gesture to B) . probably gets stopped by—(hitting finger against rim of dish and to seeking completion)

98 **B**: Yeah . the rim

99 **G**: That's what's blocking it

100 **T**: OK . now . that's— . that's reflection isn't it? That's how we see . by . light reflecting off something and coming to our eyes
Now . so we can't see that . but . tell me when to stop
(T pours water slowly into dish to cover the penny)

101 **Ss**: Stop

102 **W**: I can see it

103 **T**: The light now .

104 **Ss**: Hitting our eyes

105 **T**: is hitting your eyes
So . what has had to happen . the difference was that . after the light hit the penny . and it tried to . come out here earlier it hit the edge and it . didn't reach your eye .

106 G: <u>Oh I—</u>

107 T: <u>but</u> now what must be happening to the light?

108 G: You put the water in and it sort of like rised (makes upward gestures) . so when light hit it it went higher . and . and it hit our eyes

109 T: ⟨So that⟩ as we saw the ruler and things bending in there—
That's really what happened to this light . it was getting bent . and it gets bent so that it actually comes past the edge . and . you can see it
And that's the thing called—(seeking completion)

110 W&G: <u>Refraction</u>

111 T: <u>Refraction</u> and that's what . bending of light is

And with this simultaneous utterance of "refraction" by both students and teacher, followed by the teacher's codalike statement of equivalence, the episode comes to a close.

So What's Happening? and Some Issues for Consideration

Having examined this example of classroom interaction line by line, we are now in a position to review the episode as a whole, asking, as did the teacher when he joined the group of students, "So what's happening?" However, before attempting to answer this question, it must be emphasized that there can be no single, definitive answer. Nor is this simply a problem of the accuracy of the transcription. Rather, the problem is one which is inherent in the nature of linguistic communication itself, of which the incompleteness and possible inaccuracy of any transcription is an inevitable outcome. For just as individual moves in the discourse may be open to different interpretations by the participants who are involved in the interaction, as a result of their different perspectives on the topic and their purposes in talking about it, and also as a result of the multifaceted nature of the meaning(s) realized in the stream of verbal and nonverbal communication, so is the recorded text open to different interpretations by each person who engages with it, whether through the medium of video recording or, as here, through the medium of transcription.[8] The comments offered here must therefore be taken as tentative and disputable, being based, as they are, on one person's interpretation of the text.

Whether or not other readers of this transcript agree with the interpretation offered here, however, there can be little disagreement about the fact that it raises issues of considerable importance. Furthermore, I would suggest that, leaving aside differences due to the specifics of content, these are issues that are raised by almost any episode of naturally occurring classroom interaction. In the remainder of this section, therefore, I should like to consider briefly those that I think are of greatest significance for the topic of this chapter — the role of talk in learning and teaching.

How Much Is Learned?

One issue that should obviously be considered is what exactly the students learned from this episode. For example, one might ask whether they really reached an understanding of the principles that account for the reappearance of the penny at the bottom of the dish when water is added or, more generally, whether they achieved a sufficient grasp of the concept of refraction to be able to use it to explain other phenomena in which it is involved. On the basis of their contributions to the discussion that we have just examined, one would have to conclude that it is unlikely that either of these criteria was met.

However, to set these as the criteria for judging the success of this episode, I would suggest, would be to misunderstand the nature of the learning that is involved in a complex area such as this. It would also miss the significance of what *was* achieved in the talk that occurred, as the group made connections between their observations, their previous learning, and the problem that provided the focus for the discussion.

For it must be emphasized that learning that is concerned with understanding — rather than with the memorization of isolated bits of information or the application of a simple algorithm — is not an all-or-nothing affair. On the contrary, it involves the cumulative construction of knowledge over many encounters with relevant problems, with the learner bringing what was learned on previous occasions to make connections with the information presented in each new problem and thereby making more and better sense of the phenomena in question. This is particularly true in the present case, where a complete, scientific explanation of the reappearance of the coin requires the articulation of a whole set of theoretical concepts, of which refraction is only one. This is apparent here in the way in which refraction and reflection are first contrasted and then subsequently coordinated in the final section of the discussion. There is also a further theoretical assumption which, although never mentioned, is crucial for an understanding of both of these other concepts, namely that light travels in a straight line. Although part of the teacher's way of thinking, it is not at all clear that the importance of this assumption is recognized by all the students.[9]

It could be argued that this very complexity is a good reason for adopting a more tightly structured pedagogical mode in which the teacher introduces the necessary concepts singly and in a predetermined logical sequence. However, this makes two assumptions which, in my view, are untenable: first, that what is learned is a direct reproduction of what is taught and, second, that prior to instruction students have no theories of their own about the topic under consideration. The arguments against the first assumption have already been presented earlier in this chapter and do not need to be repeated here. However, the second deserves further consideration.

Several utterances by members of the group hint at "alternative" frameworks of interpretation (Driver 1983) being brought to bear on what they are observing, which are quite different from the "official" theory. The first of these occurs at 36, when Wendy associates reflection with putting something in water, and another occurs at 57, when she makes the correct—but in this context only partially relevant—observation that the ruler in the tank looks bigger. There is also the long sequence concerning the inversion of images on the retina, although this arises from "research" carried out as part of this unit of study and cannot be attributed to the students' understanding prior to this unit of study. However, perhaps the most interesting statement is made in the final section, when Gurmit explains what has just been observed as: "You put the water in and it sort of like rised" (108). This suggests, fairly explicitly, that this student has constructed an explanation that depends upon the notion of the image of the coin rising on the surface of the water until it reaches a height at which it once again becomes visible.

All these examples bear out the claim, made above, that learners attempt to solve problems by selecting what they judge to be relevant from what they already know to make sense of the current situation. As can be seen from this episode, such sense making is often very different from that of a better-informed person and may, indeed, appear to be wrong or misguided when judged from that perspective. Nevertheless, as Donaldson (1978) has argued so persuasively, "wrong" answers are best seen as evidence of partial or inadequate information, rather than as an indication of lack of ability or interest. One of the strongest arguments for the sort of *collaborative* sense making that is being attempted in this episode, therefore, is that it is only under these conditions that students are able to offer their interpretations for consideration by others without fear of ridicule and, in the process of discussion, to calibrate their interpretations with those of other members of the group, including those of the teacher. It is only under these conditions, too, that the teacher is able to gauge what and how the students are understanding and so to be able to shape his own contributions to the discussion so that they provide effective assistance to the students in their task of constructing a more complete and coherent understanding.

In evaluating what was learned on an occasion such as the one considered here, therefore, one should not expect to find complete mastery of the relevant concepts from a single encounter, but instead an indication that there has been a development in understanding. As one teacher commented after viewing this episode on videotape, although these students may not have achieved a full and coherent scientific understanding of refraction from this activity, they have engaged with the problem in a constructive manner and will have this rich experience to draw on when they next meet these concepts in the course of their further school learning.

But it is not only in providing an opportunity for learning about the specific topic of refraction that this episode is worthwhile. For, as I suggested above in relation to the sequence concerning the pinhole camera, there are other important lessons to be learned by the students from the manner in which the teacher handled the discussion. First, by asking the group to draw upon what they had learned from previous research as well as from their immediately preceding observations, the teacher indicated that the way in which a scientific explanation is constructed is by seeking for relevant connections between ideas drawn from a variety of situations. Second, by inviting their contributions to the discussion rather than by simply telling them the answer, he demonstrated that knowledge is jointly constructed in the collaborative meaning making that occurs as people attempt to solve particular problems. Both these lessons need to be learned if students are to become adaptable, intentional learners.

The Context of Talk

A second issue that is raised by this example is the contextual specificity of learning. Not only do the individual students bring their own current understandings to the task of making sense of this particular problem, but the manner in which the sense making unfolds is strongly influenced by the immediate situational and conversational context. In this particular case, for example, the discussion of the central problem of the penny in the dish is clearly influenced by the immediately preceding activity of experimenting with the effect of putting rulers into the tank of water. It is also influenced by the fact that the various members of the group have done some research on eyes and have made use of an encyclopedia.

Without these experiences to draw on, the students would have had less—or possibly different—ideas to contribute to the discussion.

But to put it like this is to oversimplify the way in which the context shapes the meanings that are made, and how these, in turn, create the context for what follows. To get a fuller understanding of the situated nature of understanding (see Edwards and Mercer [1987] for a discussion), it will be helpful to recall some of the exchanges that have already been considered. Let us start with the teacher's first question and the moves that follow (17–25). As we have seen, by asking "What's happening?" and by following up the students' responses with the expanded reformulation "everything's bending," the teacher implicitly creates a context in which a generalized, scientific explanation is appropriate. That is to say, he invites them to think of what's happening in a particular, scientific way. Or, to put it in terms of the Vygotskian framework adopted here, he invites them to use the ("schooled") genre of scientific explanation as a mediating semiotic tool for thinking (Bakhtin 1981; Wertsch 1991). This is made explicit early in the episode (21 and 23), when he uses the term "refraction" in his request for a definition of the phenomenon they have observed. In this sequence, then, the teacher creates the ground rules for the ensuing discussion, including the specification of the register and genre to be used.[10]

However, the discussion is not carried on exclusively in this scientific register. In fact, technical terms, such as "refraction" and "reflection" are glossed in terms of a much more everyday register, using expressions such as bending and bouncing off. And it is precisely these more familiar terms that Balkrishan draws upon, as we have seen, when he formulates what he judges to be relevant from his reading about the functioning of the eye (70). The preceding discourse thus also creates the context for what follows by making available particular linguistic terms and structures that can be assumed to be part of the group's shared understanding, since they are "given" information.

A third way in which the linguistic context can influence what is said can be seen in 57, where Wendy offers the attribute "bigger" as a completion to the teacher's immediately preceding elicitation. Of course we cannot tell whether this property of the ruler as seen through the side of the tank of water had already appeared salient to the student, but the fact that she offers it at this point can be seen to be directly related to the emphasis on changed appearances in the teacher's earlier utterance (50) and on the contrastive pattern and heavily emphasized "looks" in 56, which directs the student to construe what she had seen in terms of a changed visual attribute.

To generalize from these examples, then, we can see two main ways in which the context of preceding talk influences what follows: first, by providing a pool of words and phrases that can be drawn upon in subsequent turns, and second, by creating a conversational framework that at each point sets up strong expectations for both the form and the content of immediately succeeding moves. These characteristics of the co-construction of meaning in conversation have, of course, been commented on before, but it is only recently that attention has been given to their significance for the particular type of "instructional" conversation (Tharp and Gallimore 1988) that is being considered here.

Let us consider the patterns of discourse that are created from the point of view of repetition. When it is the students who repeat the patterns used by the teacher, this can be seen as an indication of successful modeling by the teacher of the genre-appropriate forms and meanings for making sense of the topic so that they can be appropriated by the students. According to Vygotsky (1981) this appropriation goes through two stages: the categories first occur on the social plane of group problem solving, and then subsequently they occur on the individual plane of each student's inner dialogue as he or she composes a description or report of the activity or, on some future occasion, makes sense of some similar situation through the medium of inner speech. The first phase of this mediated knowledge-construction can certainly be seen throughout this episode in the students' frequent attempts to take over and use terms introduced by both teacher and fellow students.

A second aspect of the significance of such patterning has recently been identified by Tannen (1989), who points out that both the repetition of lexical items and syntactic structures over the course of an interaction as well as the appropriate matching of adjacent moves in an exchange are simultaneously an indication of interpersonal involvement and also a group achievement. For such patterning can only be created if participants are aware of, and contributing to, the coherence of the unfolding discourse. Their occurrence thus creates "an emotional experience of insight (understanding the text) and connectedness (to other participants, to the language, to the world). This enables both participation in the interaction and also understanding of meaning" (p. 13). Other writers have made rather similar points about such patterning in terms of the achievement of intersubjectivity, which is a necessary precondition for the co-construction of meaning, and hence for the learning that occurs through talk (Rommetveit 1985; Wells 1990).

But perhaps the most important insight into the educational significance of this collaboratively created patterning of classroom discourse is the recognition that individual contributions are, to a large extent, shaped by the current demands of the group's collective efforts to build a structure of meaning appropriate to the task at hand. Each contribution is thus as much a *strategic* move, made at a particular point in the emerging discourse in response to the speaker's assessment of what is required at that moment, as it is an independent formulation of what the speaker knows or understands more generally. As a result, we can no longer treat a student's contribution to the discussion as if, as Edwards (1990) puts it, it provided a "window on the mind," allowing us to make a direct and context-free evaluation of the speaker's underlying knowledge.[11] Indeed, it could be argued that the conception implied by this metaphor of knowledge as a relatively unchanging underlying representation is itself a hindrance to our thinking about learning. Instead, we should perhaps think of learning and understanding as activities that are performed in response to the demands of specific problem-solving situations and, in the classroom, most frequently performed through contextually embedded talk.

Teacher Intervention: When and How?

In the episode that we have been examining here the teacher is clearly in control — despite the relatively small proportion of the total turns he takes. He sets the direction in his initial question and, through the language he uses, establishes the framework within which the students make sense of the problem of the penny in the dish.

Some viewers have been critical of the constraining effect of the scaffolding he provides, arguing that, despite his request for their ideas, he effectively suppresses the students' voices by offering his own account. Others have argued that, on the contrary, he gives direction to what would otherwise have been an unfocused discussion by structuring the task as a problem to be solved and by providing the language from which to build an explanation.

However, both these reactions assume that these two stances are alternatives between which a teacher must choose: either to encourage the students to make their own sense or to give them the official or textbook view. By contrast, as I have argued earlier, when learning and teaching are looked at from a sociocultural perspective, the issue is not whose version will prevail, but how to create a dialogic context (Bakhtin 1981) in which meaning is co-constructed by teacher and students together.

In such a context, the teacher remains in charge, but his or her exercise of control is manifested not in a once-and-for-all choice between intervening with the "correct" answer or standing back and leaving the students to find their own solution, but in the making of moment-by-moment decisions about how to proceed, based on knowledge of the topic, understanding of the dynamics of classroom interaction, intentions with respect to the task, and a continuous monitoring of the ongoing talk. For example, in the present case, as he listens to each student's contribution, the teacher must decide whether to make a reply that contributes to the substance of the discussion, or whether to leave the initiative with the students. And, when he does decide to intervene, he must judge whether to extend the current line of thought, nudge the conversation in what he judges to be a more promising direction, or offer support in a more explicit form, for example by supplying necessary information or by demonstrating a relevant procedure. At the same time, he must monitor group members' participation and try to make sure that good ideas are heard and developed, while still ensuring that all those who wish to contribute are given a chance to do so. In mixed groups, such as this, he must also take positive steps — for example, by looking at the girls when asking questions of the group as a whole — to overcome the cultural stereotyping that assumes boys are both more interested and more able when it comes to adopting a scientific perspective on experience.

In the present instance, it is clear that the teacher felt that intervention of a fairly direct kind was needed. But it is worth noting that, although he was anxious that the students should learn to frame the explanation for the reappearance of the penny in terms of reflection and refraction, he also listened to their suggestions and, where possible, incorporated them into the conversation. In fact, one of the most striking features of this example is the way in which he moves between everyday discourse and ways of seeing and the technical discourse of science, with its more formal ways of conceptualizing what is observed. By making a bridge between the two registers in this way he is providing an opportunity for the students to take over and internalize this "cultural tool" so that in the future they will be able to use it on their own (Lemke 1990).

However, there is one point in the episode where, from the detached and post hoc perspective of the observer, one might wish to question the form of the teacher's intervention. I am referring to the point when Gurmit is attempting to make a connection between the current problem and what he had discovered about the functioning of the eye and brain from his study of the pinhole camera. This is an example of a student struggling to construct a solution to a problem that, through a novel act of integration, goes beyond the understanding he has achieved of the separate parts. Rather than rescuing him from his difficulty by refocusing on the more limited goal of explaining the phenomenon of the reappearing penny in terms of reflection and refraction, the teacher might have intervened more effectively by encouraging the group to pursue Gurmit's line of thought a little further in order to see whether it could indeed contribute to a more comprehensive solution to the original problem. In fact, this was the teacher's own reaction when we subsequently looked at the videotape together and he added, somewhat ruefully, that that is what he would probably have done if he had been less conscious of the camera, and of the implicit injunction it seemed to convey to "stick to the point."[12]

The issue, then, is not whether but *how* the teacher should intervene. Simply setting up challenging situations and leaving the students to make what they can of them is rarely sufficient. As Driver (1983) observes; "Activity by itself is not enough. It is the sense that is made of it that matters" (p. 49). In our concern to have students take greater responsibility for their own learning, therefore, it is important that we do not mistakenly hold back from providing assistance when this is needed. On the other hand, we need to ensure that, when we offer assistance, we do so in a manner that is contingently responsive to the learners' goals and to the meanings they are constructing, and supportive of their creative attempts to make new connections and find novel solutions to problems. Whatever choice is made on any particular occasion, however, what is crucial is that the choice be perceived by both students and teacher as just one contribution to a continuing dialogue, for which they *all* have joint responsibility.

Classroom-based Research by Teachers

Discursive analyses of particular instances of classroom talk, however, are not in themselves sufficient to bring about the changes that are implied by the preceding discussion. If classrooms are to be transformed into communities of inquirers, among whose members knowledge is constructed through the talk that occurs in the course of collaborative problem solving, a different type of research will be required—research which is classroom-based and conducted by teachers to address the questions that arise from their own practice. For educational change comes about most effectively, not by the mandating of recommendations derived from academic research, but by the improvements in individual teachers' practice that occur as they carry out action-oriented inquiries with the goal of enabling them "to take defensible decisions in concrete situations" (Atkin 1991).

There are, in fact, a number of reasons for urging teachers to become inquirers who pose their own questions, conduct the appropriate investigations to find answers to them, and talk with their colleagues about the sense that they are making in the process. These reasons are implied in the theory that was outlined in the first sections of this chapter and they can be summarized briefly as follows:

- Classroom learning and teaching are always highly contextualized activities, which take place among a unique collection of individuals who each have their own personal cultural backgrounds, but who also share a history of experiences as a group. This being so, the problems that arise about how best to enact the relationship between students, teacher, and curriculum cannot be resolved by "experts" outside the classroom, for they do not know the particular context in which decisions have to be taken. The teacher, on the other hand, is the person who is best placed to take such decisions. In order to feel confident to do so, however, she or he needs the knowledge about that context that comes from systematic observation and reflection.

- People learn most effectively, not by being told what to think and what to do, but by being agents in their own learning. This applies as much to teachers as it does to any other learners. Instead of the traditional, transmission approach to professional development, therefore, which is implemented through centrally organized lectures and workshops, a new model is required which allows teachers to identify for themselves the problems that are important to them and provides the help and support that enables them to address these problems through inquiries in their own classrooms carried out in collaboration with their colleagues.

- Only when teachers have such opportunities to become active and collaborative learners about topics that they find personally meaningful and relevant will they be able to provide convincing models of this kind of learning for their students to appropriate.

Such a proposal for teachers to become agents of their own learning is neither novel nor unrealizable. Inspired by the work of such educators as Barnes, Britton and Rosen (Barnes 1969, 1976; Britton 1970; Rosen and Rosen 1973) teachers in Britain have undertaken classroom research for several decades now, often in groups organized through the National Association for the Teaching of English.

Similar projects have taken off in the United States, particularly around the learning and teaching of writing (e.g., the Bay Area Writing Project [Camp 1982], and the Breadloaf School of English [Goswami and Stillman 1987; Atwell 1990]).

However, an inquiry approach to learning and to teachers' professional development need not be limited to the curriculum area of language (Stenhouse 1975; Elliot 1991), as has been demonstrated by the very varied issues that have been addressed by teachers in the National Oracy Project in Britain (Norman, 1992) and the Talk Project in the Peel Board of Education, Ontario (Booth and Thornley-Hall 1991) from which the episode analyzed in this chapter was taken. A similar range of issues is to be found in the inquiries conducted by the teachers in the Language and Learning Project — some of which are reported in other chapters in this book — and by those who have engaged in classroom-based inquiry as part of their studies for a higher degree at the Ontario Institute for Studies in Education (Wells, forthcoming).

Whether the starting point is a very general topic, such as to find out what sort of talk occurs in group work in science (as in the episode considered above), or to explore the value of using a child's first language to help him or her benefit from a curriculum presented in a second language (Orzechowska and Smieja, forthcoming), or a much more specific topic, such as to find ways of encouraging revision of writing in the context of an environmental studies unit on living creatures (Maher, in press, see also chapter 1 in this text), the teachers I have worked with have found that action research — that is to say research that is rooted in practice and aimed at bringing about improved learning conditions through changes in practice — gives an added interest and excitement to their teaching that, in turn, brings benefits to their students. It also changes their image of themselves, both personally and professionally, enabling them to take on leadership roles in promoting the same sort of learning experiences for their colleagues in their own schools and beyond.

Not surprisingly, in the light of the arguments developed in the first part of this chapter, one of the prerequisites for this new mode of learning through classroom research most frequently mentioned by teachers who have benefited from this experience is the support of colleagues who are similarly engaged. Just as students need the opportunity to co-construct meaning in the context of joint problem solving in the classroom, so teachers, too, need colleagues in the staff room with whom to talk through the various phases of their inquiries: constructing and refining the question to be investigated, deciding on the most appropriate type of data to collect, and interpreting it once it has been obtained. But, perhaps most important of all, they need colleagues with whom to talk reflectively about the sense they are making of this new learning experience as a whole and with whom to discuss the ways in which they are changing their practice as a result of what they have learned.

For teachers and students alike, then, learning is most effective when it takes place in a community whose members carry out inquiries on topics to which they have a personal commitment and who engage in collaborative, critical, and constructive dialogue about the problems and issues that arise. It is in such dialogue that we see the true role of talk in education: in providing the means for the co-construction of meaning, from which each participant appropriates what is currently most relevant to his or her development, with the guidance and assistance of a teacher or more knowledgeable peer. In such a community of inquirers, the roles of teacher and learner are interchangeable, for all are learning and, at the same time, all are helping others to learn.

Notes

6. A further reason for the emphasis on individual achievement in education, and hence for the suspicion with which collaborative sense making is regarded, is to be found in the competitiveness that is still pervasive in public education. For example, collaboration in writing is often forbidden because it is seen as a form of cheating. It is significant, therefore, that the appeal of the current emphasis on "cooperative learning" is, for many teachers and administrators, its potential for boosting individual test scores (Johnson and Johnson 1990).

7. I have chosen to look at talk in the context of science because it is often assumed that, unlike the situation with respect to literature or social studies, there is very little room for collaborative, exploratory talk in the learning and teaching of a subject which is supposed to have such a firm basis in "fact" (see Bettencourt [1991] and Lemke [1990] for an opposing point of view).

8. Transcriptions raise problems of two different kinds. First, because of the limitations of the medium, they inevitably privilege the lexicogrammatical dimensions of utterance over the intonational, gestural, and extralinguistic dimensions, for which there are extremely limited modes of

representation. Second, in order to transcribe, it is first necessary to make an interpretation, for one can only hear what one understands (Ochs 1979).

9. I owe this observation to Allan MacKinnon.

10. For a discussion of the relationship between register and genre, see Halliday and Hasan (1985).

11. This insight has much wider implications. Written "utterances," too, whether produced as part of a curricular unit or under test or examination conditions, are strategic contributions to the discourse of the classroom community, and are shaped by the history of that discourse as well as by the implicit or explicit demands of the immediate context.

12. Dewey Dykstra made an important point, in one of his contributions to a recent electronic mail discussion, when he noted that "Good in-class conversation always looks rambling in my experience," and "I think that the "wandering" is an inevitable part of these discussions, in fact if there is no searching or critical examination then there probably is no progress, i.e., nothing new for the participants" (15 April 1991).

Chapter Three

The Literate Potential of Collaborative Talk

It is just after recess on a Thursday in February. The place a combined grade three and four classroom in an inner-city school in Toronto. Outside, although the sun is shining in a cloudless sky, the temperature is minus fifteen degrees Celsius. Inside, too, it is the arctic climate that is the focus of attention as the children engage in the exploration of self-chosen topics arising from the schoolwide theme of "The Enchantment of Winter."

The project had started for these children with a reading of Robert Service's poem "The Cremation of Sam McGee." Now, three days later, almost all of them have chosen their projects, most of them arising from the brainstorming session that followed the reading of the poem. After the initial macabre fascination with Sam's mode of cremation, it is the Yukon itself—its vast size and harsh climate that has captured the children's imaginations and most of the projects have a natural history flavor. Susan and three friends, for example, are making a study of polar bears; one of them, Siew Tin, is making a stuffed model of a bear. Seth and two other boys are finding out about wolves. Brian and Kim, two Chinese-Canadian boys, have started with an interest in maps and travel, an interest which finally bore fruit in the form of a large map of Canada and, with the help of another Asian boy, Luke, three board games involving questions about Canadian geography. Paolo is working alone on astronomy—an interest sparked by an initial question about the Yukon climate.

João and Eric started by deciding to study the terrain and, after reading in a book about three-dimensional mapping techniques,

they have decided to make a model of Dawson City and its sur-
roundings, using a photograph as a starting point. In the following
extract, they are sitting on the floor with some of the necessary
materials around them, preparing to begin the construction.

J: Eric, look!
     See, here is going to be the small mountain.
     We're going to build it up how it is in the book.
     Where's the book? (he picks it up to show it to Eric)
     You know, building it up and everything.

E: Yes

J: Here it is, see. It says "Building it up".

E: No, it doesn't mean —

J: So the small one then the big one (referring to the already cut pieces of
     cardboard).
     We can make a little river and the town on the edge too.

E: Yes, that's what I mean.

J: Yeh, OK.

E: That's what we were talking about.

J: Yes, we're starting.

E: And we can do little boats because of the little trees.

J: Yes, OK. So we have to glue this (the cardboard).

E: And these are the *****

J: Yes. No, we're not going to put a church.

E: I know I know.

J: No, we're not going to do any of that, OK?
     We are going to plan it how we planned it in the paper.

E: Yes.

J: OK, let's go.

João and Eric have already decided on their goal: to build a model
of a particular location in the Yukon. What they still have to
determine is the specific form their model is going to take and the
means for achieving it. This extract forms part of the process of
reaching shared understanding, which is essential if they are to
engage in joint action. So, despite its limitations, it is an example of
the sort of talk that we wish to concentrate on in this chapter. We
shall call it *collaborative talk*. However, before going on to discuss
this and other similar extracts from the recordings that we made in
this classroom, we wish to explain our reasons for singling collaborative talk out for special attention from all the other kinds of talk
that occur in a typical classroom.

The Role of Talk in Active Learning

Let us start by stating our assumptions about learning and the role that interaction plays in learning. To do so, we must first make a distinction between the learning that is involved in coming to be able to recall relatively isolated items of information, and the learning that is involved in the acquisition and development of more complex conceptual structures and cognitive procedures. It is primarily with the latter type of learning that we shall be concerned, since it seems to us that to understand and make provision for this is likely to bear productively on the former, but not vice versa (Anderson 1982; Pascual-Leone 1980).

The learning that is essential to cognitive development, we want to argue, is most likely to occur from engaging in activities in which it is necessary to recognize and solve problems of increasing levels of difficulty. In order to tackle a problem — particularly one that one has not been encountered before — it is necessary to be able to represent it to oneself in such a way that one is able to generate and choose between alternative means to its solution and then to carry out the procedures that one has judged likely to be effective. It is important to recognize that this is not a simple, linear procedure, however, since at any stage feedback on success so far or information not originally available or seen to be relevant may call for revision of some aspect or, indeed, of the whole procedure. In our own field, this recursive nature of problem solving has been most fully explored in relation to writing (e.g., Flower and Hayes 1981; de Beaugrande 1984), but there are good reasons to believe that essentially the same principles apply in any kind of problem solving and thus they are of very general applicability in thinking about the provision of opportunities for the type of learning with which we are concerned.

Not everybody will be happy with this emphasis on learning as occurring in the course of conscious and deliberate problem solving. On the one hand, in early childhood, there must be some doubt as to how far mental activity is amenable to conscious control; indeed one of the major objectives of early education is to help children to develop reflective awareness of their own mental processes (Donaldson 1978). And on the other hand, the learning that takes place as a result of listening to a story, for example, may hardly seem to involve either problem or solution. However, insofar as reading or listening involve an active construing and interpreting of the text, it does not seem entirely inappropriate to assimilate them to a problem-solving model, which is clearly appropriate for the vast majority of activities in which children engage both in and out of school.

For learning of the desired kind to occur, however, it is not sufficient simply to organize a program of activities in which problems may be encountered. First, the learner must play an active role in selecting and defining the activities, which must be both challenging and motivating; second, there must be appropriate support. Let us consider these two requirements in turn.

The first requirement is that the activities chosen should make demands that are in certain respects at or just beyond the limits of the learner's current capabilities; the demands should also be such that the learner is willing to engage with them. Where individuals perform tasks of another's devising, carrying out procedures according to someone else's instructions (for example, writing a project report for which the structure and major section headings are provided by the teacher), there is little need for the application of critical intelligence in defining and planning the task or in executing it effectively. The more challenging aspects of the task have already been taken care of by the expert, and so the opportunity for the learner to develop that expertise is denied by the organization of the task itself. However efficient it is in ensuring the production of acceptable outcomes, therefore, the distribution of responsibility for task performance that vests control in the teacher is not well adapted to the development of knowledge and control by the learner.

Recognition that the construction of knowledge is an active process that each individual learner must carry out for him or herself (Wittrock 1974), on the other hand, has led to a greater emphasis being placed on what has been called "ownership" of the activities through which learning is intended to take place. This requires that learners be given a share in the responsibility for selecting the tasks in which they engage, for deciding on the means to be employed in carrying them out, and for evaluating the outcomes. Only in this way, it is argued (Barnes 1976), can they gain an active understanding of the principles involved and of the procedures that may be effective in achieving the desired outcome. A further, not unimportant, reason for encouraging the learner to take ownership of the task is that it increases his or her motivation to find and carry out a means of completing it successfully.

It nevertheless remains true that in many cases the learner will not be able successfully to carry out the whole task unaided. The second requirement, therefore, is for appropriate support. This means support that is related to the particular difficulty experienced and that is made available at the time when it is needed. The organizational difficulties that this requirement may seem likely to present are typically circumvented in the teacher-directed curriculum by breaking the activities in question into small steps and providing clear instructions on how each is to be carried out. In this way, the occurrence of difficulties is reduced to a minimum. However, as has already been argued, the consequence of such an approach is that the opportunities for active learning are also drastically reduced.

However, rather than seeing difficulties as something to be avoided, we should look at them as providing ideal opportunities for facilitative intervention. This, as we understand it, is what Vygotsky (1978) meant when he argued for engaging with the child in "the zone of proximal development." In contrast to Piaget (at least in his early work), Vygotsky saw the development of higher cognitive functions as originating in interpersonal interaction, through which the learner appropriates the knowledge and expertise that is made available in the support provided. In the words of his best-known formulation, "What the child can do today with help, tomorrow he will be able to do alone."

What Vygotsky meant by this rather cryptic remark is spelt out in more detail by Wertsch:

> When children come to a point in an activity that proves too difficult for them, they turn to an adult for help. The activity is then carried out on the interpsychological plane. The future development of the child with regard to this activity consists of gradual transference of links in the activity's functional system from the interpsychological to the intrapsychological (i.e. from the *social* to the *individual*) plane. The activity then becomes an intrapsychological function, since the child is capable of directing his/her own attention to the elements in the environment that are necessary for carrying out the task (1981, p. 30).

This, of course, is not a complete explanation. Exactly how the "transference" takes place still has to be spelled out in detail and, as Bereiter (1985) points out, we are still very far from having a satisfactory account. Nevertheless, while we may not be able to explain *how* learning takes place, there is little doubt that the availability of relevant models at the moment when they are needed has an important part to play. Equally important is the help that a collaborative partner can provide in enabling the learner to marshall and exploit resources he or she already has available, but over which he or she does not yet have explicit and conscious control (Karmiloff-Smith 1979).

The major role of interaction in learning, therefore, is that it provides the chief means through which the teacher can enable students to learn from engaging in activities that pose problems to be solved. We shall now go on to argue that, in this context, collaborative talk optimally meets the requirements just discussed.

Enabling and Empowering Learning

So what is collaborative talk? Conceived quite generally, collaborative talk is talk that *enables* one or more of the participants to achieve a goal as effectively as possible. This may, as in the opening example, be a goal involving action, such as making a model or buying the right number of rolls of wallpaper to paper a room. On the other hand, the goal may be much more abstract, such as understanding a scientific principle or planning a piece of research. Or it may involve the interplay between thought and language that occurs in writing as, for example, in the compilation of a set of instructions or in the composition of a paper to be delivered at a conference. The occasions for collaborative talk may thus be very diverse. But what they all have in common is that, at some level of specificity, one of the participants has a goal that he or she wishes to achieve and the other participant engages in talk that helps the first to achieve that goal.

In most cases, the participants in collaborative talk are of approximately equal status, each able to take either of the roles of principal actor or facilitator and to benefit accordingly. Typically, too, the purposes of the collaboration are achieved when the task is completed or, at least, when the principal actor is able to continue with the next step. The talk has then served its instrumental purpose and, in the light of the effectiveness of this outcome, can be judged to have been more or less successful. This was the case in the extract from the two boys' discussion quoted above, just as it was in the collaborative talk that preceded and accompanied the preparation of this chapter. And the potential value of such enabling peer collaboration should not be underestimated.

However, the benefits of collaborative talk need not be limited to the function of facilitating achievement of the task. Where one of the participants has greater expertise than the other, he or she can engage in interaction with the learner about the task with the deliberate intention of enabling the learner to acquire some procedure, knowledge, or skill that will be useful in other situations beyond that in which he or she is currently engaged. In these cases, collaborative talk not only facilitates the task, it also *empowers* the learner. Indeed, we do not think it would be too strong a claim to say that, under ideal conditions, it has the potential for promoting learning that exceeds that of almost any other type of talk. It is the ideal mode for the transaction of the learning-teaching relationship.

For collaborative talk to have this empowering effect, however, it must meet two essential conditions. The first of these has already been addressed: it must be based on the assumption that the learner has ownership of the task and the teacher must strive to ensure that this ownership is respected. In practice, of course, ownership is a matter of degree, for the learner may not yet have sufficient confidence to take full responsibility for every aspect of the task or the necessary executive procedures for planning and carrying it out. A major objective of such talk will, therefore, be to help the learner to develop conscious and deliberate control over his or her mental processes, not only in order to complete the task in hand, but also so that he or she becomes progressively more able to take responsibility for his or her own learning more generally (Bereiter and Scardamalia 1989).

The second essential condition arises from the first: the expert's contributions to the dialogue should be "contingently responsive" to the needs of the learner (Wells 1986), as these needs are understood in the light of the immediate situation as well as of the longer term goals of education. To date, there has been little mention of this important characteristic of interaction in discussions of teacher-student talk, although its importance is clearly recognized in studies of much younger children. Schaffer (1977), for example, considers the contingent responsiveness of a caretaker's interactive behavior to be essential for the infant's earliest social and intellectual development. In studies of language acquisition, too, the same quality has been found to characterize the conversational style of parents whose children are accelerated language learners (Cross 1978; Wells 1985a). The content of adult-child conversation changes, of course, as the child increases in competence and experience. However, the learning process is continuous, as are the conditions that facilitate it. At every stage, the same conversations that provide the basis for the child's acquisition of the language system also simultaneously provide evidence about the way in which the community makes sense of experience and about how the resources of language can be used for thinking and communicating. Therefore, since there is no reason to believe that there is any radical change at the age of school entry in the basic strategies that the child uses to learn from the evidence provided in such conversations, there is equally no reason to believe that contingent responsiveness ceases to be the feature of adult contributions that best facilitates the learning process.

Thus, whether in incidental learning situations in the home or in the more deliberate situations that teachers arrange in the classroom, the principles that should guide the adult's participation in collaborative talk are essentially the same. Adapted from Wells (1986), they can be stated as follows:

- Take the child's attempt seriously and treat it as evidence of his or her best effort to solve the problem unaided.
- Listen carefully to the child's account and request amplification and clarification as necessary to ensure that you have correctly understood.
- In making your response, take the child's account as a starting point and extend or develop it or encourage the child to do so him- or herself.
- Select and formulate your contribution in the light of the child's current manifested ability as well as of your pedagogical intentions, and modify it, as necessary, in the light of feedback provided by the child.

Put much more succinctly, these principles can be summed up in the injunction to "lead from behind." What is important is that it is an understanding of the learner's conception of his or her task and of the way in which he or she plans to set about it that provides the basis for the teacher's decision as to how best to help the child to progress from where he or she is now towards the more mature understanding and control that the adult already possesses.

When the requirement for contingent responsiveness is met, collaborative talk can fulfill its empowering function. Not only the learner is empowered, however; so also is the teacher. For it is precisely through frequently engaging in collaborative talk that the teacher is able to increase his or her understanding of children's thinking in general (Duckworth 1987), and it is *only* by engaging in such talk with a particular learner while he or she is engaged on a specific task that the teacher can become knowledgeable about that learner's purposes and current state of understanding, and thus be able to make his or her contributions contingently responsive to the learner's needs.

The Characteristics of Collaborative Talk

So far we have looked at collaborative talk in very general terms, considering the contexts in which it is likely to flourish and the conditions that must be met if it is to empower learning. Now we wish to examine the nature of collaborative talk more closely in order to identify those characteristics that promote the sort of reflective and systematic thinking on which such learning depends.

In order to achieve the benefits of having two minds focusing collaboratively on a problem, the participants must achieve intersubjectivity in their representation of the task in hand and of their proposals for dealing with it. Each needs to know the other's under-standing and intentions, and both must take the appropriate steps to ensure that mutual understanding is maintained. There is a need, therefore, to be explicit. Thus, in order to explain the matter in hand sufficiently clearly for the other participant to make an informed response, each is forced to construct a more coherent and detailed verbal formulation than would be necessary if he or she were working on the problem alone. In the process, gaps and inconsist-encies become apparent and can be repaired, with the result that the problem is seen with greater clarity.

However, it is not only the adequacy or inadequacy of the offered information that is revealed in these circumstances, but also the connections that are made between the parts. In developing the account, the role of cause-and-effect relationships, of inferences, generalizations, extrapolations, and so on, is also made apparent, as are failures to make such connections. In sum, the need for mutual understanding in collaborative talk requires each participant to make his or her meaning clear to the other, and hence also to him- or herself, with the result that thinking is made explicit and, thus, available for inspection, and, if necessary, for extension, modifi-cation, or correction.

Then, having achieved a shared understanding of the task, par-ticipants can now, from their different perspectives, offer opinions and alternative suggestions. Once again, there is a need for explicit-ness. But more importantly, opinions and suggestions need to be justified and supported by relevant arguments, and reasons need to be given why one alternative is more appropriate than another, if decisions are to have a principled basis. As a result, participants in collaborative talk can not only learn from each other's differing knowledge bases, they can also learn the need for disciplined thinking and develop some of the strategies for achieving it.

Depending on the stage reached by the principal actor in the execution of his or her task, the collaborative talk may focus on any one or more of the following components: specifying the goal more precisely, planning the means for achieving it, generating and choosing between alternatives, reviewing achievement to date, or modifying what has been done.

Choices and Connections: Collaborative Talk in One Classroom

In the first part of this chapter, we have been concerned with giving an idealized account of collaborative talk and with justifying our claim for its preeminence as a mode of teacher-learner interaction. However, we want to acknowledge immediately that the ideal conditions that we have assumed in the theoretical discussion are rarely encountered in reality. There are three main reasons for this. First, the sheer number of children who need to be supported, and the constraints imposed by the organization of the school day, mean that many interactions are cut short or interrupted. Second, since most of the children work in small groups rather than individually, there are issues of group collaboration to be addressed as well as the substantive issues raised by the tasks themselves. Third, there are limits to the resources of personal knowledge as well as of books, materials, and equipment that the teacher can draw on immediately in meeting the needs of particular children as they arise spontaneously in the course of the day. For all these reasons, the ideal can rarely, if ever, be achieved.

In turning to an examination of examples taken from one particular classroom, therefore, we wish to make it clear that our purpose is not to evaluate them, but rather to explore the potential of collaborative talk as it is conducted in practice. To do this we shall focus our discussion of the extracts on the following four questions:

- In what ways is the talk collaborative?
- What aspects of the task are addressed in the participant's talk?
- What aspects of learning are being enabled in the talk?
- How are the participants contingently responsive to each other?

"So you've changed your topic."

Let us return to João and Eric. In the extract below, they have not yet begun to construct their model. As the teacher joins them, the two boys in their enthusiasm both start speaking at once:

1 J: <We're> doing a model

2 T: <u>Wow</u>

3 E: <u>I know</u> what the model's going to be
(João and Eric both talk at once for eight seconds as they describe their intentions, so neither can be heard)

4 T: Hold it! I hear that you're making a model. I hear something about houses.

5   What's this going to be about? What's your topic?

6 J: Yukon

7 E: Yukon

8 T: You're making—
   (João and Eric again speak together making the next few lines difficult to understand)

9 J: In the Yukon they have shops . I saw it in the *

10 E: You can make—you can make igloos

11 J: They say they have shops ** and it has a big mountain beside it

12 E: (to Richard, who has come to look) And we can do the other side **

13 T: So you're going to do a little town?

14 J: (nods)

15 T: Wow!

16 J: And we could make a big mountain and <put those things> on top

17 T: Uh-huh uh-huh

18 J: And then it would be covered with snow

19 T: Uh-huh

20 J: And then um—we could make a little shop here and park

21 T: What questions are you answering particularly?

22 J: Um—...Like "Where did they get the name from?" so we wanted—we wanted to do the model

23 T: So you—you've changed your topic a little bit

24   So you're making a model of the Yukon . showing a town?

25 J: Yeh

26 T: And some of the things you've learned about what it's like to live in the Yukon, is that it?
   (During the next few turns Eric is trying to secure T's attention by calling her name. He has been left out of the preceding discussion)

27 J: But the mountain is small for the size of the town . like the mountain *-

28 T: Which town is this?

29   Is it a particular town?

30   D'you know the name of it?

31 J: It's the Yukon

32 T: That's the name—that's the name of the big territory

33   Can you find the name of a town?

34 E: We don't know
   (T hands book to João and talks to Sandra briefly while João and Eric consult the book)

35 T: OK (turning back to boys)

36   This is a map that shows very few towns

37   There's one

38 J: I know . Whitehorse

39 E: <u>Whitehorse</u>

40 T: Whitehorse . that's a famous . town in the Yukon

41   Uh-huh . Whitehorse

42 J: Is Alaska there too?

43 T: Pardon?

44 J: Alaska Alaska (pointing to two occurrences of the name on map)

45 T: This is the Alaska Highway — the Alaskan Highway

46 J: It's very complicated because it says United States and then the
United- it's over there see

47 T: Yeh

48 J: The United States and <u>then United States</u>

49 E: <u>**</u>

50 T: OK . Why might it be like that?

51   Do you understand why?

52 J: Maybe . it's the <shore's down that *> too?

53 T: Yeh Alaska belongs to the United States

54 S: (who is on the edge of the group also looking at a map) I found it I
found it

55 T: You did?

56 E: (looking at index) It says Yukon — Yukon's three things and ** you
can find — you can look through every page . that has the Yukon in it

57   One of them might be a photograph of a town

58 T: That's true that's true

The first point to note is the teacher's "active listening," indicated
in the opening lines by her "Wow!" and "I hear that you're making
a model," etc. By echoing what the boys have said, she is assuring
them that she has heard and is interested. She is also letting them
know what she takes to be the salient points in what she has heard
and indirectly inviting them to consider whether these are the
points that they, too, judge to be the most important. At the same
time, the particular phrasing of (4), "I hear something about houses,"
suggests that there is some problem about comprehensibility — a
problem to which the solution might range from being more informative or explicit to speaking one at a time.

The teacher's first turn ends with a question about the issue
that underlies their decision to make a model: "What's this going to
be about? What's your topic?" (5). Although their first replies seem
to provide some sort of answer, it is clear from what follows (9 − 20)
that they have not really understood the purpose of her question.

For the two boys continue to elaborate on the details of the model they want to make rather than considering the question to which their model is addressed. In spite of this, the teacher continues to listen and echo back to them (e.g., "So you're going to do a little town" [13]).

But interspersed with her expressions of support, she continues to address the problem of articulating a statement of inquiry by posing questions that might elicit the issue the boys are investigating: "What questions are you answering particularly?" (21), and "So you're making a model of the Yukon . showing a town? And some of the things you've learned about what it's like to live in the Yukon, is that it?" (24—26). This last question, it will be noted, also acts as a model of the sort of question which the boys' intention to construct a model could appropriately address.

By juxtaposing these two kinds of response, the teacher is making a critical distinction for the children between the action-goal, that of making a model, and the topic-goal, that is to say, the question that is directing their inquiry. This is clearly an important distinction for them to understand, for it is only when the two goals are brought into interaction with each other that an inquiry can be productive. Moreover, it is a distinction that is too often overlooked in discussions of goal setting with students, although it has begun to figure in recent research on writing (Freedman 1985).

That her concern is with the need for an articulation of a statement of inquiry rather than that they should stick to a previously agreed topic is corroborated by the teacher's ready acceptance of the change that has taken place: "So you—you've changed your topic a little bit" (23). At the same time, this observation also emphasizes the teacher's recognition of the boys' ownership of the task and her willingness to accept their decision to change their topic. In so doing, she also demonstrates another important feature of planning: that the setting and revising of goals and subgoals is an ongoing and recursive process as the various components interact with each other.

In fact, the following talk (28—61) exemplifies the revision of planning in operation, as the agreement that the model will be of a single town rather than of the whole Yukon Territory leads to a scaling down of the original intention and to the search for a specific town to be the subject of the model. With the help of the book provided by the teacher, Eric comes up with a strategy for solving the problem (56—57), and it is by using a photograph of Dawson City that they are able to form the specific plan that is being discussed in the extract with which this chapter opened.

"I think he's got a point."

During the next week, the model progressed apace and, by the time we meet João and Eric again, they are reaching the final stages.

1 J: We're going to — we're going to cover it with white tissue paper, Eric

2 E: \<That's what we've got to do\>

3   That's for when they have snow .

4   And after . by mistake it could avalanche on here (pointing to the base of the mountain on the model) and some houses will be crushed

5 T: I wonder if that's a danger here (pointing to the equivalent place on the photograph)

6   I think you're quite right about some <u>mountains</u>

7 J: <u>I thought</u> it was summer (in the photograph)

8 E: Yeh but in winter — but if it's in winter . .

9 J: Yeh . yeh the seasons could change

10 T: That's true

11   And they don't move their houses here <u>. .</u> do they?

12 E: **

13   Yeh they can't like lift it and go "ow ow" (miming lifting a very heavy weight) unless they just go "da da da da" (said in a sing-song voice, which seems to represent the use of magic)
(all laugh)

14 T: I don't think they're going to do that . .

15   Well if you have a look here . . (pointing to photo in book)

16   See where the houses are . along the river . and then .

17   What does this look like?

18 J: That's a mountain

19 T: Part of the mountain

20 E: (pointing to model) These are one of these mountains

21 T: Uh-huh uh-huh

22   You know you don't have to have the same number of houses in here as in the photograph (pointing to book)

23 E: <u>I know</u>

24 J: <u>Yeh</u> but some of — like one or two over here would be OK (pointing to base of mountain on model)

25 E: Yeh but if we put one or two over next to the houses . we won't have room for the tissue paper

26   Here almost squashed even

27 T: Right . sounds like this is something you boys have to talk about a little more

28   You both have good points

29 J: Yeh I think he — he got a point because . if we put tissue paper over it . that —

30 T: Is that what you plan to do with these houses?

31 E: Yeh

32 J: And then we could put like . little — put it like little streets coming through here

33 T: Uh-huh . interesting

34 E: Yeh we could like er . if you still want to make the thing, right? we could make — you could put pine trees all around there

35 J: Around the mountains

36 T: Very good

37 J: OK, let's go

As is evident in this and the earlier extract, collaborative talk emphasizes both the personal and the social aspects of learning. The social is made important because successful completion of the task depends on the combined efforts and expertise of both participants; the personal, because each collaborator has his own resources, ideas, and approaches to the task. But most importantly, the commitment to collaborate obliges the participants to recognize the relevance of each other's expertise and, where necessary, to realign their own knowledge systems. It is this balancing of the social and the personal that enables learning to occur.

From a superficial reading of these transcripts, it might appear that, of the pair, it is João who plays the dominant role of knower/ doer and that Eric is the helper. However, a closer examination of their talk, particularly the extract currently under consideration, makes it evident that each has his own ideas about the task of making a model of Dawson City. It is not surprising, therefore, that their differing perspectives should come into conflict when, as in this extract, they have to reach a practical decision on how to proceed. However, it is not their differences that are noteworthy. Rather, it is the way in which collaboration on the task to which they have committed themselves both brings out each child's differing abilities and makes it possible for each to enable the other's learning in the joint thinking and doing that the task demands. As the teacher commented on reading the above extract, "These two boys have a fascinating style of working through their [mis]conceptions with a lot of talk that appears confusing on the surface but on reflection their logic is evident."

The nub of the problem is that João wants their model to be an accurate representation of the scene in the photograph from which they are working, while Eric is more concerned with achieving internal consistency within the model itself. The problem is brought into focus by the question as to whether they should add more houses to the model. Based on the number he can see in the photograph, João wishes to site some more at the foot of the mountain. But, following through the implications of João's plan to use tissue paper to represent snow on top of the mountains, Eric argues that, if an avalanche were to occur, houses placed at the foot of the mountain would be crushed (3−4). Although João accepts this objection, he does not abandon his plan for, a moment later, he again suggests adding more houses at the foot of the mountain (24). This time Eric counters with the objection that if the houses were too tightly packed together, there would not be room for the tissue paper that they intended to put on the roof of each house (25−26) and to this practical (i.e., constructional) objection João agrees and concedes that Eric has "got a point" (29). They could, however, represent streets going between the houses (32) and, in place of the houses at the foot of the mountain, Eric suggests, they could put pine trees (34). With this agreed, the practical João calls for a resumption of activities: "OK, let's go."

To this interaction, it is interesting to note, the teacher contributes very little by way of suggestion or new information. It is as if, as she herself put it in a subsequent discussion, her presence is sufficient to enable the two boys to listen to each other's perspectives and take account of the arguments behind them. And this is the impression one gains from examining her role in the discussion. She listens to what each of the boys has to say and, in her responses, implicitly accepts the validity of both points of view. "I wonder if that [i.e., an avalanche] is a danger here," she says to Eric (5), pointing to the foot of the mountain in the photograph — the spot that is in dispute as the site for additional houses on the model. But João's wish to achieve an accurate representation of the photograph is also recognized when she tells them that they don't have to have the same number of houses in the model as in the photograph (22), and she states "You both have good points" (28).

In this respect, her most interesting contribution to the discussion is line 11. Perhaps sensing that João has not fully appreciated the implications of Eric's argument, the teacher jokingly points out that people in the Dawson City shown in the photograph do not move their houses with the changing seasons and, therefore, by implication, that even if their model depicts a summer scene, they should take account of such a hypothetical winter catastrophe by not siting houses in a position from which they would have to be removed if they were to change their model to represent the same scene in winter. It is not possible to tell from the ensuing remarks whether the two boys took in the full significance of this one utterance, the force of which depends on the initial "and" that makes connection with João's preceding concession that the seasons could change, and the "here" that contrasts the city in the photograph with the boys' representation of it in the model. The point we are making, however, is not that this utterance succeeded in convincing João, but rather that it illustrates very clearly the teacher's concern both to make her contributions contingently responsive to each of their perspectives and, at the same time, to encourage them to follow the incompatibility of their implications through to a logical conclusion. As she says a moment later, "Sounds like this is something you boys have to talk about a little more" (27).

Conclusion: Attaining Literate Thinking Through Talk

The preceding analyses of the collaboration between João, Eric, and their teacher have illustrated the potentially empowering nature of collaborative talk and have highlighted the centrality of concerns such as problem solving, ownership, challenge, and intersubjectivity of understanding. If we now look at the list of characteristics that are intrinsic to the achievement of these concerns — such features as explicitness, connectivity, justification, and relevance — it will be seen that they are precisely the sort of attributes that are held to be particularly characteristic of written discourse (Chafe 1985). They are also attributes of thinking that are considered to develop as a consequence of becoming literate (Cole and Bruner 1971; Goody 1977). Since, however, we are dealing here with spoken language, it seems that we should reconsider the traditional definition of literacy and, in the present context, ask what "literate thinking" is and how it develops.

Until quite recently, answers to these questions would almost certainly have taken for granted that the linguistic-cognitive processes of reading and writing must be centrally involved (e.g., Olson 1977). However, as a result of further comparisons of spoken and written language, including cross-cultural studies (Scribner and Cole 1981; Heath 1983a; Tannen 1985), a more complex picture has begun to emerge. While it would probably still be agreed that literate thinking is most likely to occur in connection with reading and writing, it is now recognized that thinking that displays many of the same characteristics can occur in oral interaction between those who are literate when the purposes of the interaction demand it (Olson and Astington 1990). Langer (1987) cites the following example:

> When a group of people read one of the classics and then discuss the theme, motives, action and characters at a Great Books meeting, I would say they were using literate thinking skills. ... Further, when those people see a movie and then discuss the motives and alternative actions and resolutions, I would again say they were using literate thinking skills even though they had neither read nor written. And if the people engaged in that very same conversation about a movie did not know how to read or write, I would still say they had engaged in literate thinking (p. 3).

If we accept this argument, then we must also accept that the process of becoming literate can potentially take place through speech as well as through engagement with written language. For it is not the mode of language use that defines literate thinking, but rather the manner in which the language is employed. Thinking is literate when it exploits the symbolic potential of language to enable the thought processes themselves to become the object of thought. Under appropriate conditions, this can occur in either writing or speech.

Throughout this chapter, it has been assumed that the prime function of schooling is to develop effective thinking. We can now make this assumption more explicit by stating that what schools should be attempting to promote is the development of *literate* thinking. Elsewhere, we have argued for the preeminent role of writing in performing this function (Wells and Chang 1986; see chapter 3 in this volume), although we would have to concede that not all writing has this effect (Wells 1987). However, even when giving primacy to writing, we have also made a plea for the recognition of a similar role for talk, while recognizing that it is only certain types of talk that have these literate consequences. In this chapter, our aim has been to show that one type of talk that has this potential is what we have called collaborative talk. It now remains to show just how this can occur.

As an example, let us consider the discussion between João and Eric of their reasons for and against locating more houses at the foot of the mountain in their model of Dawson City. Both boys have to make their arguments explicit; they also have to make them relevant to their own position as well as to that adopted by the other. Although these requirements are reduced somewhat by the physical presence of the objects referred to, there is no doubt that they are felt and, within the children's capabilities, responded to as well. Decisions concerning relevance and presentation thus come into play, and these are certainly instances of literate thinking.

Another important aspect of literate thinking is the recognition of the need to consider alternatives and to justify them by appeal to systematic knowledge. This, too, is illustrated in the collaborative talk between João, Eric, and their teacher when each has to extrapolate from his or her knowledge about seasonal variation in climate, topography, land relief, and so on, in order to decide whether to site more houses at the foot of the mountain. Although the discussion is brief, it illustrates how the collaboration that is necessarily involved in a task such as making a model can lead children purposefully to access their mental dictionaries of knowing and understanding and, in the process, become more aware of them.

Reflecting on what one has done — questioning the outcome of one's efforts — and revising it, if necessary, is another important feature of literate thinking. For the testing of one's assumptions of knowing and not knowing may lead to, or at least call for, a realigning of or adding to one's existing knowledge systems. Although this kind of literate thinking is a common characteristic of expert performance, it is one that has to be deliberately acquired (Bereiter and Scardamalia 1987). Encouraging children to question their own efforts is one way of helping them to adopt this practice.

So far, we have drawn attention to the literate consequences of addressing the content of the task: the need to make one's intentions and one's understanding of the topic intelligible to another and at the same time to oneself. But we should also recognize the potential benefits that derive from the goal-oriented nature of collaborative talk. The tasks in relation to which the talk occurs make demands for planning and execution, which themselves may become the subject matter of talk. It is important to emphasize, however, that it is not the talking through of plans that is claimed to be advantageous in itself; rather, it is when planning and similar processes are raised to the level of conscious attention so that they may be brought under intentional control that such talk warrants being described as literate.

A good example of this conscious attention to goal-setting occurs when João and Eric are asked to formulate the question they are addressing in the making of their model. This episode qualifies as literate, we would argue, because in responding to the request to identify their question, João and Eric are developing self-regulatory procedures. They are learning to adopt a "What is my question?" and "Where am I going?" stance to the task they undertake.

Of course, thinking of the kind that we have characterized as literate does not only occur when activities are carried out collaboratively. It might also have occurred if the children in this classroom had been working on their own, although it would probably have been in an attenuated form. However, because they needed to achieve intersubjectivity about their intentions, which was essential if their joint efforts were to be productive, the children were encouraged to turn their thinking back upon itself—reflectively selecting and evaluating it—in order to construct an intelligible, coherent, and convincing verbal formulation. It is above all because it can foster the growth of this critical reflectiveness that collaborative talk has such important potential for the development of literate thinking.

In this chapter, we have only had space to consider two examples of collaborative talk, taken from recordings made in the course of one class project—although further examples are to be found in other chapters in this volume. As a result, there is a danger that we have read more into what was said than the participants themselves were aware of. We must also admit that our claims about the potential benefit of collaborative talk may not have been realized in the learning that actually took place as a result of these particular interactions. On the other hand, although of limited significance when considered in isolation, the extracts that we have analyzed take on a different significance when they are seen as a small but representative sample of the many similar learning opportunities that each child enjoyed during the course of those two weeks.

However, it is with the teacher's comments that we should like to end. They are taken from a discussion that followed a viewing of that part of the recording that included the first discussion with João and Eric.

> That part with João and Eric—it's just like that business that kids need time to talk about what they're going to write about, to work out their ideas, and then to do rough copies to find out what they really think, and then revise. . . . That really interested me. I kept seeing little parts where it's like João and Eric—that nudging them to make the connection between two ideas, asking them what their topic is. I mean it's the same as the writing process—having them tell you what they're doing, where they're going, what their questions are . . . and having them review the process and what they're doing.

Attending to the extracts that we had selected to analyze, the teacher has clearly made a very similar interpretation, understanding and knowing for herself the significance of the talk in which she had been involved. Although she does not use the term herself, there is little doubt that what has excited her about these examples, and others like them, is the potential for the development of literate thinking that is to be found in collaborative talk.

Chapter Four

Language in the Classroom
Literacy and Collaborative Talk

As in the preceding chapter, the central concern here will be with the relationship between talk and literate thinking. However, first I want to raise some more general questions about the place of talk in the classroom: who engages in it, under what conditions, and for what purposes? There have been repeated calls during the last twenty years or so to give a greater place to spoken language in the classroom. Taken at face value, however, this seems a rather strange injunction, since classrooms have rarely been places from which spoken language is absent. In the typical school day, as study after study has shown, approximately two-thirds of the time is taken up with speech. To be sure, the very same studies have also shown that two-thirds of the speech that is officially sanctioned is produced by the teacher, so that, as far as any individual student is concerned, the proportion of time that he or she is permitted to speak is only about 1 percent of the total day. Certainly, therefore, there is a need to rectify this imbalance by bringing about a change in the way in which speaking rights are distributed. Teachers need to listen more and to talk less, and individual students need to have more frequent and more substantial opportunities to contribute productively to classroom interaction.

However, simply to increase the amount of talk in the classroom may not bring about a significant improvement either in language learning or in learning through language. More important than the quantity of talk, it seems to me, is its quality: the type of interaction to which it contributes and the purposes that it serves in students' overall learning experiences (compare Corson [1988] for an extended discussion of these issues). In the following sections, therefore, I shall consider some of the areas in which there may be misunderstanding concerning the role of spoken language in the classroom, as a prelude to arguing for one particularly important type — that which we have called collaborative talk.

One argument that I have often heard for an increased emphasis on spoken language is that it will provide a way of overcoming the linguistic deficiencies of those children from lower-class and ethnic minority homes who do not have an adequate command of the language of the mainstream society that is used in the classroom. However, stated in these bald terms, the diagnosis does less than justice to this complex issue. In the first place, it would in most cases be wrong to consider children in either group to be suffering from a language deficit. Research on first language acquisition has shown that, whatever their social background, by the age of school entry, all but a very small minority of children have acquired a basic mastery of their first language and are able to use their linguistic resources to engage in conversations on a wide variety of topics and for a wide variety of purposes with the members of their immediate community (Wells 1985b). If the linguistic resources of these children or the uses to which they habitually put them do not match those of the classroom, this becomes a handicap only when these resources are rejected as inappropriate and the children themselves treated as inadequate.

However, it would also be a mistake to equate the two groups. Whereas the monolingual children may still have to learn the genres of language use that are particularly valued in the classroom, this may not be the case for the child who has to learn the language of the school as a second language. Depending on his or her home experiences — and, in some cases, previous schooling in the country of origin — equivalent genres may already be relatively familiar, although in another language. In either case, what is important is to discover which ways of using language are already familiar to each individual child — avoiding making assumptions based on class or ethnic stereotypes — and to value them and use them as far as possible as the basis for the further learning that is necessary for full participation in the curricular activities of the classroom (Heath 1983b).

If the diagnosis is too simplistic, so is the proposed remedy. For children of lower-class origin, the question is not one of mastery of the language per se, but rather one of the uses to which it is typically put. Such children have little difficulty in communicating orally with each other, either in or out of the classroom, and so merely to increase the proportion of time devoted to peer interaction is unlikely to be of great benefit to these children. Nor is a simple increase in the amount of student-teacher interaction. For, as has repeatedly been shown, much of the talk that typically occurs under teacher direction is more concerned to shape student behavior, both verbal and nonverbal, towards some notional standard, than to encourage the clear and vigorous expression of personally held values and opinions (Barnes 1969; Edwards 1992; Hammersley 1981).

For children who are learning a second language, more talk may not be particularly beneficial, either. For an emphasis on spoken language, without some further specific purpose in view, is likely to lead to a focus on mastery of language form for its own sake. Even when the declared intention is the development of communicative competence, this is unlikely to lead to mastery of the genres necessary for full participation in curricular activities, unless there is equal emphasis on the content that is being communicated and on the necessary thinking processes.

A further danger in emphasizing spoken language for its own sake is that it may lead to a restriction in the opportunities for access to written language. Indeed, the argument is sometimes put forward that these so-called linguistically disadvantaged children are not able to benefit from encounters with print because of their lack of command of the language, and that they therefore need compensatory experience in the oral mode instead. Unfortunately, this diagnosis can persist indefinitely so that, even after several years in school, when they have started to be taught to read and write, they may still be considered unable to cope with activities that involve sustained reading and writing and continue to be given oral language activities to "prepare" them for the encounters with written text that remain forever in the future. However, as is becoming increasingly clear, these reading and writing competencies can only be acquired through actually engaging in sustained reading and writing (Edelsky 1986; Langer 1986), which is precisely what they are being denied. Furthermore, both reading and writing lead children to discover and make use of vocabulary and structures that they would be unlikely to meet in speech. Ironically, a well-intentioned emphasis on spoken language can actually deprive children of the linguistic experiences of which they are most in need.

This leads me to the second of my reservations, namely that the dichotomy that is made between spoken and written language is not, from an educational point of view, the important one. Instead, what we should be asking about any language event in the classroom is, Does it enhance the development of literate thinking?

The Centrality of Literacy

The term *literate thinking* as I am using it here, refers to all those uses of language in which its symbolic potential is deliberately exploited as a tool for thinking. This is a relatively new way of conceptualizing literacy and one for which there is as yet no simple term in most languages. Bruner (1972) provides a helpful gloss when he describes literacy as "a cognitive amplifier" and notes that written language is the most powerful technology generally available for the empowerment of mind.

Historically, the invention of writing has had far-reaching consequences. By providing a means of giving a permanent representation to the thoughts expressed in speech, it has altered the nature of information storage and retrieval, making it possible for the accumulation of knowledge to be independent of the limits of human memory (Goody 1968). This has been of immense importance in the development of Western civilization, for almost all our cultural institutions—religion, law, science, and so on—are founded upon the cumulative structure of experiences and ideas that are recorded in writing.

But what I wish to emphasize in the present context is the potential of this invention for the intellectual life of individual members of a culture in which this technology has a central role. Texts of various kinds not only make the accumulated knowledge and experience of the culture readily available, but their very existence as fixed verbal formulations facilitates the making of the crucial distinction between what was actually "said" (the fixed text) and the various interpretations that can be derived from it. As a result, readers can be encouraged to attend to the actual propositions that are asserted, to evaluate their coherence and consistency, and to examine the evidence adduced to support them and their plausibility in the light of their own experience. This treatment of linguistic formulations as entities that can be examined and evaluated also leads quite naturally to the development of a metalanguage for talking about texts and about the thinking associated with their production and interpretation (Olson and Astington 1990).

Encounters with written texts thus have the potential to encourage the development of a discriminating, critical response, in the course of which readers may extend and sharpen their understanding of, and deepen their response to, the matter concerned. At the same time, they also tend to promote a more reflective attitude to the relationship between experience and the linguistic propositions—and choices between them—that are used to encode it.

What has just been said about interpretive and reflective reading is even more true of writing. For, unlike reading, which leaves no trace of the mental processes in which one has been engaged, writing creates a record that is the outcome of those processes. What one has written can be critically read, in the same way as a text by another person, in order to see what it means; it can also be rewritten, in order to develop ideas that were initially unclear or incomplete. Thus, by writing, reading, and rewriting, and by discussing one's text with others, one can work on one's own thinking in a conscious and deliberate manner (Murray 1978).

From the point of view of intellectual development, therefore, what is important about reading and writing is not so much the communication of information, as the possibility of developing ways of using language as an intentionally controlled tool for thinking and feeling. However, although this type of literate thinking may have arisen historically as a result of the use of written text, it is no longer *dependent* on the activities of reading and writing. When the appropriate conditions arise, literate people can "speak a written language" and such literate behaviors permeate a great part of their everyday life, as they plan their activities and review and interpret events in the light of their concerns, beliefs, and expectations. Thus, worlds of experience — whether real or imaginary — that are created through words may be apprehended, explored, and connected through literate thinking in speech as well as in print.

If literate thinking is so central to the lives of many adult members of our society, it is not surprising that it should emerge as the prerequisite for success in education. In the Bristol Study, "Language at Home and at School," measures of reading, writing, and study skills were found to be the core of general school achievement when this was assessed at the end of the elementary stage of education. And when we searched for the antecedents of this achievement, we found that the two single most powerful predictors were the children's measured reading ability at the age of seven and the place and value accorded to literacy in their parents' own lives, with these two measures together giving a multiple correlation of $r = 0.91$. Projecting still further back into the children's early experiences, the most powerful predictor of reading ability at seven was the children's knowledge of literacy on entry to school ($r = 0.82$), and that in turn was significantly predicted by the frequency with which they had stories read to them in the preschool years ($r = 0.55$). From this analysis there thus emerged a cluster of results around the central thread of literacy — results which certainly implicated the activities of reading and writing, but in contexts which also included talk about the texts that were read or written (Wells 1986).

In recent years, there has been considerable confirmatory evidence of the long-term educational value of reading stories to children in the pre-school years (compare the summary by Teale [1984]). Equally, the educational disadvantage that results from a lack of this experience is documented by Heath (1983b), particularly with respect to the children from the lower-class black community that she labeled Trackton. What emerges clearly from these studies however, is that much more is involved in sharing stories with children than simply a familiarization with the structures and vocabulary that are characteristic of written language and a growing facility in handling the layout and conventions of print. For it is in the talk that typically accompanies the reading of a story that children are encouraged to explore the imaginary world created by the words of the writer and to relate it to their own experience, noting and making explicit the similarities and differences. That is to say, it is in the talk about the text that they begin to develop that characteristic stance towards the relationship between language and experience that in our culture has been particularly promoted by the inventions of writing and print (Olson 1986).

While the shared reading of stories may be the most powerful literacy-promoting experience for the pre-schooler, it is by no means the only one to be found in literate households, as has been shown in a number of recent studies (e.g., Goodman 1984; Schieffelin and Cochran-Smith 1984; Taylor 1983; Tizard and Hughes 1984). Indeed, Heath (1986) has reported a decline in the frequency with which American youngsters have stories read to them. Apparently, parents are too busy driving their children to ballet classes, hockey practices, and scout activities to have time simply to stop and read. But, as they speed along the highways, they ask their children to pay attention to the sights that they pass, to give accounts of what they have been doing, and to justify the decisions they have made. In other words, these children are being initiated into those literate modes of language use that support literate thinking through events that are transacted in speech.

Heath (1986) refers to these types of oral literacy events as "genres of language use," and she identifies six that she considers to be crucial for subsequent success in school. In what follows, I give an abbreviated quotation from her exposition.

1. Label quests. These are language activities in which adults either name items or ask for their names.

2. Meaning quests. Within this language activity, adults either infer for the young child what he or she means, interpret their own behavior or that of others, or ask for explanations of what is meant or intended.

3. Recounts. Within this genre, the speaker retells experiences or information known to both teller and listener. As children retell, they may be questioned by the listener who want to scaffold the telling in a certain way.

4. Accounts. Unlike recounts, which depend upon a power differential, where one party asks another to retell or perform for the sake of performance, accounts are generated by the teller. Accounts provide information that is new to the listener or new interpretations of information that the listener already knows.

5. Eventcasts. In this genre, individuals provide a running narrative on events currently in the attention of the teller and listeners, or forecast events to be accomplished in the future.

6. Stories. This is perhaps the most familiar genre, because of our customary associations with the written stories read to children and requested of children's imagination. The mold of these fictional accounts is such that they must include some animate being who moves through a series of events with goal-directed behavior (pp. 168−70.)

As Heath and others have shown, some or all of these genres can and do occur in homes of children from all social classes and all ethnolinguistic groups. But research also shows that there are substantial differences between homes in the relative frequency with which these genres occur and in the importance that is attached to them. The result is that children come to school with different degrees of familiarity with the literate behaviors that have been found to be so central to full participation in those classroom learning activities that lead to successful achievement. And it is in this respect, rather than in a more general familiarity with the language used in the classroom, that some children may find themselves disadvantaged when they come to school.

Nevertheless, teachers who are alert to this problem can do much to reduce its long-term effects by identifying the sorts of literacy events with which individual children are familiar and by providing opportunities for them to engage in those events that they may not have encountered at home. This will indeed involve much use of spoken language. But not just interested social chat; not talk that is deliberately set in opposition to reading and writing. Rather, it will involve contexts and activities that give rise to genres of language use in which speaking, listening, reading, and writing are integrated in order purposefully to engage in literate thinking about topics and texts that both children and teachers find meaningful and significant.

What sorts of classroom contexts and activities are most likely to give rise to such events? In order to answer this question, we need to look in more detail at the relationship between language, learning, and teaching.

Language, Learning, and Teaching

During the last half-century, our understanding about the nature of knowledge and its acquisition has undergone a major revolution. As a result of work on cognitive and linguistic development by such researchers as Piaget (Piaget and Inhelder 1969), Bower (1974), Brown (1973), Donaldson (1978), and others, it has come to be recognized that, far from being passively received, all knowledge has to be actively constructed by each individual knower as a result of his or her interactions with the external world. What can be learned, and hence what knowledge will be acquired, depends at each stage on the learner's resources of existing knowledge; it also depends on the strategies of meaning making that the learner can bring to bear on the evidence that is made available in the situations in which he or she becomes purposefully engaged.

At the same time, because so many of our purposes involve other people, the way we come to make sense of situations — and thus the knowledge we construct — is strongly influenced by others through the coordinated mutual interpretation of each other's intentions, as these are realized through action and speech (Newson 1978; Vygotsky 1978; Wood 1988). Thus, although we can no longer think of children as passive recipients of knowledge that is transmitted in a prepackaged form to them by others, we do not need to abandon the notion of teaching. Instead, we have to reconceptualize it as *behavior that has as its intention to facilitate the active construction of knowledge by the learner.*

Unfortunately, this conception of the relationship between learning and teaching — and of the role of language in actualizing this relationship — has been slow to influence what happens in school. Partly as a result of the pressure of numbers and of the directives that are received from outside the classroom in the form of curricular guidelines, and partly because of their own experiences as learners, teachers tend for much of the time to work in a manner that is almost diametrically opposed to the needs of learners and to the way in which knowledge is typically constructed outside the classroom.

Although some of our learning is conscious and deliberate, in everyday life the greater part of it occurs incidentally in the course of achieving our various practical purposes. One of the major aims

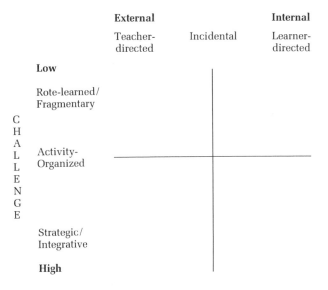

Figure 4–1
Challenge and Control in learning.

of education, on the other hand, is to help us to become more systematic and reflective in our learning. Schooling is not only about constructing new knowledge; it is also about deliberately seeking connections that will integrate different areas, and developing strategies that will enable us to exploit our existing knowledge to maximum effect. Unfortunately, a great deal of what is actually required of children in school lacks this challenge, consisting as it does in the learning by rote of relatively arbitrary and isolated skills or items of information. Furthermore, while the declared aim is to encourage students to become independent, self-motivated learners, much of their actual experience in school emphasizes external control and dependence on teacher authority and expertise.

These contrasts can be represented schematically, as in figure 4–1. In terms of the two major dimensions of challenge and control, most everyday learning is located at or around their intersection. Classroom learning activities, on the other hand, tend all too often to be low in challenge and high in external control (the top left quadrant). This is in direct contrast to the expressed goals of education, which stress high challenge and internal control (the bottom right quadrant). The need, therefore, is to find ways of creating classroom conditions that will enable students to develop intentional, strategic, and integrative control of their own learning (Bereiter and Scardamalia 1989).

On the basis of the ideas about learning briefly sketched out in figure 4−1, it would seem that such classrooms will share certain essential characteristics. First, the activities that are undertaken in them will in general be problem-oriented and will allow for alternative possible solutions, with the choice between them being an essential part of the task. Second, there will also be activities that encourage the making of connections between different areas of knowledge and experience. Third, there will be opportunities for students to take initiative in the selection and definition of tasks; they will also be expected to assume responsibility for making and carrying out decisions concerning their execution. That is to say, they will have ownership of their own learning tasks.

Although the first three characteristics emphasize the provision of opportunities for students to be active constructors of their own knowledge, this does not mean that there is no longer any requirement for teaching. However, as argued in chapter 2, these characteristics call for a different type of teaching. Its emphasis should be less on instruction, assessment, and control, and more on the provision of guidance and support that is contingently responsive to the immediate needs of students as they undertake the activities that have been jointly negotiated and as they strive to find solutions to problems that they have had a part in formulating. The fourth characteristic of such classrooms, therefore, is an enactment of the learning-teaching relationship in a manner that enables knowledge to be co-constructed by students and teachers together.

It is hardly necessary to add that the talk that occurs in the performance of such problem-solving activities has a central role to play in the sort of classroom I have been describing. Not as an end in itself, of course, but as the means whereby learners and their peers and teachers interact with each other as they negotiate the tasks to be carried out and collaborate with each other in making sense of the ideas and operations involved in their execution.

In the remainder of this chapter I should like to discuss one example of this sort of collaborative talk, in order to illustrate how it arises from, and provides support for, the kind of challenging, learner-directed activities that have just been discussed.

Co-constructing Meaning in Collaborative Talk

The example I have chosen is taken from the same combined grade three and four class that was described in the previous chapter, in which, over a two-week period, the children worked on self-chosen topics within the broad theme of winter and the Yukon. The unit had started with a reading of Robert Service's ballad, "The Cremation of Sam McGee," which paints a vivid picture of the harsh climate of the Yukon. Not surprisingly, therefore, in the brainstorming session that followed the second reading of the poem, many of the questions that the children suggested for investigation had to do with the weather and its effects on human and animal life. The teacher then suggested that they should form small groups according to the topics that interested them most and set about planning and carrying out their chosen investigation. The deadline for the whole project was a parents' evening in the middle of the third week, by which time each group was expected to have produced some representation of what they had learned.

The topics finally selected were varied and, in some cases, involved considerable modification of the question initially proposed. However, in all cases, the teacher encouraged them to think out for themselves the questions that they wanted to answer and the methods they were going to use, since how to find and develop a topic that was both interesting and challenging, while still being within their capabilities to address, was part of what she wanted the children to learn in the course of this unit. Once their topic was selected, the teacher also expected them to work for the most part without direct supervision. She also met regularly with each group to discuss their progress and to help them to find ways of overcoming the problems that they encountered. She also tried to be one step ahead in anticipating and providing the sorts of resources that they might need, such as reference books and construction materials.

As has already been mentioned in chapter 2, many of the children had been fascinated by the description of the intense cold that had been the death of Sam McGee and had asked questions about climate and weather. Marilda was one of them and, in partnership with her friend Jacinta, she had begun to work on the climate of the Yukon. This had led to an interest in the wind, which Marilda had been following up by reading about simple experiments on wind that she could carry out in *Scienceworks*, a book produced by the Ontario Science Centre (1984). Following the directions in the book, she had made a simple weather vane by pinning a drinking straw onto an eraser at the end of a pencil (with a small bead between straw and eraser), and then fastening a paper clip on one end of the straw and a rectangle of cardboard on the other. She had taken her weather vane into the playground during the midmorning break and demonstrated its working to her friends. Back in the classroom, she had discovered that an effect similar to that caused by the wind could be produced by blowing at the weather vane. As she had observed, the weather vane pointed to the person who was blowing.

At the point when we join her, Marilda is proudly demonstrating her weather vane to her teacher.

1 M: Miss * (trying to attract T's attention during ten seconds)

2 It's here my windfinder

3 T: OK so here's your windfinder

4 That's a good name for it isn't it?
(Marilda blows wind finder)

5 Eric, have you seen this windfinder?

6 E: Yes last year we were studying about it

7 T: Uh-huh

8 (to Marilda) Can you explain- can you explain how it works?

9 S: (who is passing) Yes I know how <u>it works</u>

10 E: ***

11 T: Oh I—I—excuse me Eric I was really—I was really talking to Marilda

12 (to Rosa) Maybe you'd be interested in this. Do you want to come over here?
(Several other children have gathered round, including Jacinta and Maggie)

13 M: When you—when the wind blows—it's trying to find the wind

14 When the wind blows this points to which direction it's coming from (pointing to the pointer on her windfinder)

15 J: Yeah like * (taking the windfinder and blowing at it, causing the pointer to point at herself. She has done this several times before with Marilda)

16 M: <u>See it points round to you</u>

17 T: <u>Why's it pointing to you?</u> (referring to Jacinta, but addressing the question to the whole group)

18 E: Cos she's the one who blew . and if you keep um —
(Maggie tries blowing)

19 J: You have to blow hard
(Maggie blows hard)

20 M: OK now blow again
(Maggie blows again)

21 M: It stays in the same spot cos- <u>cos the wind's-</u>

22 T: <u>Why?</u>

23 J: Cos it needs a big surface to blow on . to push it

24 T: Come on (encouraging Marilda to continue)

25 M: Cos the — cos the wind's blowing that direction and <u>it</u> —

26 J: <u>No</u>

27 <u>Why did it go?</u>

28 M: —it's <u>not coming</u> in a different way

29 E: Because it doesn't have a piece of paper over here (pointing to the pointer end)

30 J: **

31 T: <u>What would</u> happen if you had a piece of paper over there?

32 M: It'd turn around?

33 J: Because it needs a big surface to blow on to push it .

34 T: So it's —

35 E: And that's a big surface

36 T: So it's got something to do with the surface of the paper?

37 Ss: Yeah

38 T: And the air?

39 E: Mm

40 M: And the — this thing . maybe (pointing to the bead, which acts as a washer)

41 T: Oh and —

42 E: <u>It's the needle</u>

43 J: <No I think it's got to turn->

44 E: It's the needle . it's the needle that — well not the needle but the . <u>the straw</u> . it's the straw has the hole

45 M: This makes it —

46 E: The straw has the hole and the hole like causes it to . to make a wiggly turn

47 T: Yes (somewhat doubtfully)

48 E: **

49 M: <u>No it's this</u> that makes it-

50 T: Which? the bead?

51 M: Yeah

52 T: The bead . you think the bead is very important?

53 M: Yeah

54 T: Why? Why do you think that's important?

55 J: Let's <u>try it</u> without the bead

56 M: Cos the-

57 T: That's a good idea . that — that would . be a way of finding out if it's really important

58   First why do you think the bead's important?

59 M: Well—

60 E: It's a nuisance

61 M: —some machines they have—the little round things

62 E: Yes but some machines <u>don't have them</u>

63 T: <u>Ballbearings?</u>

64   You mean ballbearings

65 M: Yeah . so maybe like it might make it—might help by spinning it . like spinning

66 T: It's got something to do with the spinning and then making it easier to spin

67   I like your idea Jacinta . that's a very interesting idea taking the bead out

68   I don't know whether Marilda would . want to do that now or not

69 M: OK I'll try it (she and Jacinta go away to try the experiment)

Marilda is clearly proud of her achievement in constructing the windfinder and seizes every opportunity to demonstrate it to others. She is also intrigued by its operation. It is entirely natural, therefore, that she should choose to share her achievement with her teacher, rather as a writer shares his or her first draft with a sympathetic reader. "It's here, my windfinder," she says. And looking at the construction, the teacher not only shares her pleasure, but also expresses her geunine interest by asking her, "Can you explain how it works?" (8).

Several other children have gathered round, so the task that faces Marilda is a complex one. First, she has to make connections between her personal experience of constructing and using the windfinder and what she knows about the principles of its operation, acquired from her reading and other sources; second, she has to select from what she knows about the key elements that will enable other people to share her understanding; and, finally, she has to express that information in a way that takes account of her audience's needs as listeners. Indeed, when the cognitive demands of the task are set out in this way, it is easy to see why having to explain what one knows to someone else can be such a stimulus to the clarification and organization of that knowledge and, in many cases, to the discovery of the gaps in what one knows that one needs to fill in order to give an adequate explanation.

In fact, this is what seems to happen for Marilda, as she attempts to meet her teacher's request. Her first attempt stays at the level of observational description: "When the wind blows, this points to which way it's coming from" (13–14). Although accurate as far as it goes, this response does not really address the question of *why* the windfinder behaves in the way it does. To answer this question, it is necessary to appeal to the principles that underlie the observed movement of the pointer. And it is to this level of response that the teacher's further probes (17, 22) are directed. At first, Marilda does not seem able to reply. Perhaps she does not understand the sort of answer that is required. That would seem to be the implication of her next two attempts (21, 25). Or perhaps she has difficulty in selecting that part from what she does know that would be an appropriate answer. Whatever the nature of her difficulty, she listens to the other children's attempts and to the teacher's summary (36, 38) and, by 40, is able to contribute a further element to the developing explanation.

What is particularly interesting about Marilda's contribution at 40 is its tentative nature. Although colloquially expressed, it has the function of a hypothesis, and it is this that Jacinta picks up in her suggestion that they try an experiment to discover whether the presence of the bead is important for the functioning of the wind-finder. The teacher is quick to recognize the value of the suggestion (57) but, before encouraging the two girls to carry out the experiment, she attempts to find out the grounds on which Marilda has based her hypothesis. And, in responding to these probing questions, Marilda finally shows that she is indeed able to move towards the level of principled explanation.

Looked at as a whole, this episode is interesting from a number of points of view. First, it provides a good example of how a spontaneously occurring event—Marilda's demonstration of her windfinder—can be "problematized," in this case by the request for an explanation, and thereby made an occasion for intellectual growth, both for Marilda and for the other children who contribute to the explanation. When Marilda fails initially to answer in explanatory terms, the teacher helps to make the problem explicit, but she does not take over the responsibility for providing the solution. Instead, she allows the other members of the group to join in and, in the turns that follow, although there is a considerable amount of overlap between them, it is clear that they are not merely competing to give the most acceptable answer. They are also listening to each other and building on each other's contributions. This is most obvious in Eric's addition to Jacinta's statement:

Jacinta: Because it needs a big surface to blow on to push it

Eric: And that's a big surface (pointing to the card)

At the same time, the teacher contributes by restating and summarizing what they have said, but with a questioning intonation, which does not give her stamp of approval, but rather seeks their agreement for her formulation of their ideas. The result is that the explanation that is constructed is not the work of a single individual — and certainly not the authoritative statement of the teacher — but the collaborative achievement of the whole group. It is thus a very clear example of that co-construction of meaning, which is the hallmark of collaborative talk.

Second, as she accepts Marilda's observational description, makes it the starting point for exploratory talk that leads to a restatement of the observed facts in terms of explanation, and then pursues one aspect towards the empirical testing of a hypothesis, the teacher enacts with the children the basic cycle of scientific inquiry: observe, theorize, hypothesize, observe. Almost certainly this demonstration was not deliberate, in the sense of being pre-planned. However, its incidental nature does not make it any less valuable. For, in the long term, it is spontaneously arising experiences of this sort, in which the logical structure of explanation grows out of a narrative account, that will provide the children with a basis on which to construct the more abstract understanding that the activity of scientific inquiry requires (Bruner 1986).

Finally, both in her contingent responsiveness to Marilda and in the way in which she plays her role in the enactment of the cycle of inquiry, we see her empowering her students to become intentional learners as she creates the conditions for a classroom community of inquirers. Although better informed than the other members of the group, she is willing, as she put it in a subsequent discussion, "to learn with the children," neither abandoning her responsibility to ensure that each becomes more skillful and knowledgeable, nor falling into the error of believing that the only way to teach is to tell.

But let us end the discussion of this episode with Marilda. Following the attempted oral explanation and the subsequent experiment, Marilda went on to write about the windfinder and to carry out further experiments on the wind. One of these formed the substance of a demonstration that she prepared for the parent's evening. For most of the evening she was standing by her display to explain it to anyone who would stop to listen. But for those who happened to show an interest when she herself was not present, she prepared the following tape-recorded message; she also hung a written version of it above her display.

Where does the wind come from?

If you want to know where the wind comes from, use a lamp without a shade and corn starch. Only 89 cents plus tax. Use a lamp as the sun. Now for the exciting part. Turn the lamp on for three minutes. Then put a pinch of corn starch above the lamp and drop it over the lamp and it starts to rise. Then PRESTO! it disappears like that.

— By Marilda and Denise

Like many of the children in her class, Marilda has discovered an interest that is extending her knowledge and challenging her to develop her thinking. She is also developing control over the genres of language use that are necessary for the communication of her thinking, whether in speech or in writing. However, perhaps the most important thing she is learning is that she, too, can be an expert with information that others want to learn. When it is added that Marilda's first language is Portuguese and that, at the end of the previous year, her achievement level had been such that she had not been promoted to the next grade with the rest of her peers, we can see how much she has achieved. We can also see what is meant by the empowerment of learners by a style of teaching that values the kinds of literate thinking that can be achieved through collaborative talk.

Conclusion

I started this chapter by arguing that simply to increase the amount of spoken language in the classroom would not significantly improve the learning opportunities provided for students unless there were also radical changes in the quality of classroom talk and in the purposes that it served. In particular, I argued that to place an emphasis on spoken language for remedial or compensatory purposes might well be counterproductive. For teacher-controlled exchanges, in which items of information or of language form are taught and tested independently of activities oriented towards goals that students have made their own, do not constitute an effective method of enabling students to develop competence with respect either to linguistic communication or to curriculum content.

However, there is no justification for such a compensatory view of language education, as the notion that, by reason of their membership in nonmainstream ethnic and cultural groups, a substantial proportion of children are ill-prepared to meet the language demands of the classroom has been shown to be a myth. Nevertheless, it is a myth that has retained credence amongst educators because, rather than reexamine their cherished ideas about the appropriateness of the language demands they make on their students, they have placed the blame for failure to meet these demands on the students themselves and on the communities from which they come (Cummins 1984).

Fortunately, however, some teachers have started to question the appropriateness of the language demands made in teacher-directed classrooms, as they have observed their students at work and discovered abilities and interests that they had not previously known to exist (Barnes 1976; Goswami and Stillman 1987; Jaggar and Smith-Burke 1985; Pinnell and Matlin 1989; Norman, 1992). As a result, in their various ways they have begun to change their classrooms, and the activities in which people engage within them, to create communities of collaborative inquirers. In these classrooms, language is less a subject to be taught than it is a set of resources to be drawn upon in carrying out the various activities necessary to conduct an inquiry and communicate the results to others. Under these conditions, there is no need to make a plea for more spoken language, since talk is the medium in which collaboration naturally takes place, as students and teacher generate and set goals, plan the necessary actions, carry out their inquiries, and discuss ways of representing what has been discovered so that it can be shared with others. Nor is a sharp boundary drawn between spoken and written language, since all four modes of language activity — speaking, listening, reading, and writing — together with doing and thinking, perform complementary roles in the achievement of the overall goal of the inquiry.

In the latter part of the chapter, I have discussed one example selected from among many similar episodes that were observed in one such classroom. In it, we have seen how the collaborative talk that arises in the context of activities that are oriented towards goals of understanding, construction, and presentation of student-owned topics both enables children to make progress towards those goals and provides opportunities for the development of more general strategies for effective problem-solving. Collaborative talk thus contributes to those aspects of students' linguistic and intellectual development that are essential for success in school — and indeed, for success in life beyond the walls of the school — by enabling them to extend their control over those particular genres of language use that contribute to literate thinking.

For those who believe that such challenging tasks can only be undertaken by the most able, mainstream children, it is perhaps worth pointing out, in conclusion, that the majority of the children in this classroom come from lower-class, ethnic minority communities, in which a language other than English is the main medium of communication. The implication, I think, is clear. Where the aim of the teacher is to facilitate each individual's construction of knowledge through literate thinking and collaborative talk in the context of student-chosen topics of inquiry, all learners will be empowered, whatever their social or ethnic background.

Chapter Five

Creating Classroom Communities of Literate Thinkers

Fri, Jan, 8, 1988. Frist day

Hi my name is Margarida and I live at 38 Redford St. Today at school we got assigned to an animal. We have lots of animals in are class room. She gave as numbers and I was number 5. I got to be a mely worm. I said I hated mely worms. But then I said to my self maybe it will be kind of fun!

Mon Jan 11 1988

Today I fil more better about the mealy worms and I studeyed it a lot and I did have fun I had lots of fun.

Tues Jan 12 1988/−Wed Jan 13

Today I said I wonder if I feed the mealy worms some pizza and see if they will eat it. Anyway I tink thet they are going thro a stage my techer said she has a booklet and she is going to let me read it.

These are the first three entries in the learning log that Margarida kept over a six-week period, during which her whole grade four class made a study of animals, their habitats, behavior, and modes of reproduction. For some of the time, Margarida worked in a group of three, observing and recording the metamorphosis of the mealy worms. For part of the time she worked more or less independently on a study of the panda, the results of which she presented to other children in a number of sharing sessions at the end of the project. Throughout the six weeks, Margarida also spent part of most days in discussions that involved the whole class. Some of these arose around books and objects related to the animal themes that were introduced into the classroom workshop by the teacher or by the children. Others involved a reflective consideration of the activities that the children were engaging in and of the strategies that they were developing for making sense of their experiences. The ways in which Margarida learned and collaborated were typical of the kinds of learning engagements and transactions that her teacher encouraged and supported for all the children in the class.

During this period, the authors of this chapter were also engaged in research in the same classroom. Ann Maher, the teacher, wanted to discover whether children's skills as inquirers and writers would be enhanced if the processes they engaged in were made explicit through class discussion. Wells undertook to videotape some of the activities that took place in order to provide evidence for Maher's inquiry. At the same time, the observations that were made contributed to the larger longitudinal inquiry in which both Chang and Wells were engaged, since six of the seventy-two children in that study were in Maher's class.

In this chapter we intend to examine some of the collaborative events that occurred during this project on animals. Our aim will be to explore in depth the sorts of opportunities for learning that they provided and, by relating these examples to issues of practice, to develop a rationale for the transformation of classrooms into communities of collaborative inquirers. But first we need to set out the three principles that have led us to propose this mode of organizing learning opportunities as a more effective alternative to the traditional mode of knowledge transmission.

Knowing and Coming to Know

Let us start with *knowledge*, the acquisition of which is, by common consent, the major purpose of schooling. According to the *Concise Oxford English Dictionary* (sixth edition 1976), knowledge is "the state or condition of understanding [some matter], acquired by learning." Unfortunately, however, the provisions made in many schools for students' attainment of this state of understanding have been seriously hindered by misunderstandings among educators about the conditions under which it can best be achieved. These stem, in large part, from mistaken views about the nature of knowledge itself. Since, explicitly or implicitly, these misconceptions have been so pervasive in public education, it is important that we start by trying to achieve a clearer understanding of the way in which knowledge is constructed by individuals and within a community.

Because the outcomes of individuals' mental processes can be given external representations through symbolic systems such as language, music, or mathematics, and because these representations can be stored in physical objects such as books, journals, maps, or floppy disks, it is easy to believe that these objects actually contain knowledge. And, from there, it is a short step to acting as if knowledge can be given to somebody in the same way as the book or map can itself be given. However, such a belief is entirely erroneous.

First, knowledge does not exist in packages that can be transmitted from one person to another. Being a state of understanding, knowledge can only exist in the mind of an individual knower. And it has to be constructed—or reconstructed—by each individual knower through a process of interpreting or making sense of new information in terms of what he or she already knows. Even when something is said to be "common knowledge," all this means is that, within a particular community, individual members each have a representation of that event or state of affairs and believe that every other member of the community has a similar or equivalent representation. Furthermore, the acquisition of knowledge is more appropriately conceived of as an organic process of making meaning than as one of passively receiving it. It is for this reason that those who have studied the acquisition of knowledge, such as Piaget (1977) or Bruner (1972), have emphasized its active nature, preferring to characterize the process of coming to know in terms of "construction" instead of "accumulation."

Second, to emphasize the individual, constructive nature of knowing and coming to know is not to deny nor ignore the importance of the social dimension of the process. To be sure, certain types of knowledge arise mainly from an interaction between an individual and his or her physical environment, such as the acquisition of conservation, studied by Piaget. But for most types of knowledge, interaction with other people provides an essential input to the process of construction (Vygotsky 1978). In conversational interaction, participants formulate linguistic representations of their understanding of the matter in question and modify those representations in the light of the feedback they receive in the contributions of other participants on the appropriateness of their formulations. Conversation can thus provide a forum in which individuals calibrate their representations of events and states of affairs against those of other people, and realign and extend their existing mental models to assimilate or accommodate to new or alternative information. In this way, knowledge, although residing in individuals, has the possibility of being exposed to social modification and of undergoing change and revision. As Bruner and Haste (1987) emphasize, what is involved is a *dialectical* relationship between the individual and the social.

Third, within such an account of the social context through which knowledge is constructed by the individual, there can be little place for an absolutist interpretation of the notion of "truth." If knowledge is true belief, as philosophers have argued, true must be taken to mean either "verified against personal experience" or as "being in conformity with the beliefs of others as these have been publicly expressed." It cannot mean true in an absolute and final sense since, as we have already seen, every individual's knowledge is open to revision and, as the history of science amply attests, even some of the most strongly held theories have been supplanted by others that have been judged to give a better explanation of the available evidence.

But what, it may be asked, does one's conceptualization of the nature of truth have to do with the provision of opportunities for learning in the classroom? Our answer is that, even though they may remain tacit and unexamined, educators' beliefs about the relationships between truth, knowledge, and learning are of profound importance, because they underpin their concepts and expectations of schooling and of the orthodoxy by which school-based learning should be governed. Unfortunately, as is illustrated by one authoritative pronouncement after another, the methodologies of teaching at all levels of education are still to a large extent based on implicit beliefs in the absolute nature of knowledge and in the feasibility of the transmission of this knowledge from expert to novice. Such methodologies, furthermore, accord little significance to the active, constructive nature of learning or to the role of social interaction in the processes whereby each individual comes to know. This brings us to the second issue that needs to be addressed: the relationship between individual learning and the modes of interaction that are practiced in the classroom.

Learning Through Interaction

Linguistic interaction plays a crucial role in the process of learning whenever that learning is dependent on the incorporation of information that cannot be obtained exclusively from the individual learner's transactions with the physical environment. Traditionally, and particularly in high schools and universities, the typical mode of interaction is that of the lecture, that is to say, of an extended monologic exposition of a topic, often interspersed with sequences of display questions (i.e., questions to which the questioner already knows the correct response). In this mode, an expert presents his or her knowledge to the learner, who is expected to be both willing and able to receive it. This can be represented diagramatically as:

Expert −−−−−− [knowledge] −−−−−−> Novice

Although extended exposition has an important part to play in the totality of classroom life (in generating interest in, or providing a preliminary survey of, a topic to be addressed, or in summarizing or recapitulating what has been learned), it is totally inappropriate as the dominant mode of interaction. For, in this mode, little or no provision is made for students to contribute *their* interpretations and reformulations as well as whatever expertise they have, since the underlying orientation is typically that of knowledge trans-mission. Thus, it is not difficult to understand why frustration and boredom among learners are likely to occur when extended expo-sition is the dominant form of interaction in classrooms.

To give due recognition to the active and constructive role of the learner, a different mode of interaction is required—one in which the expert and the learner see themselves as fellow members of a learning community in which knowledge is constructed collab-oratively. Here, the underlying assumption is that each participant can make a significant contribution to the emerging understanding, in spite of having unequal knowledge about the topic under study. The relationship can be represented as follows:

It is important to point out that the difference between these two modes of interaction—the transmission-oriented and the collab-orative—does not lie in the spatial arrangement within which the expert and the learners find themselves, although there is a general correlation between the spatial arrangement and the discourse gen-erated. Rather, it lies in the nature of the discourse itself, which arises from the way in which the participants relate to each other and to the topic that they are addressing. In other words, in a situation in which the expert stands in front of a group of learners, collaborative learning can still prevail; just as, in instances where expert and learner are seated side by side, a transmission orientation may nevertheless characterize the ongoing interaction.

Within the collaborative mode, it is necessary to highlight two further characteristics. First, the teacher does not always assume expertise and authority about the topic under inquiry. One desirable consequence of this is that it opens up the class to pursuing topics that the students find challenging and intriguing but that may be beyond the teacher's knowledge repertoire. The emphasis, instead, is on encouraging students to discover and pool their expertise, and it is the teacher's adoption of such an emphasis that enables individual learners within the group to contribute meaningfully to the ongoing inquiry. Thus, in collaborative settings, the distinction between expert and novice is no longer statically maintained, but is subordinate to a concern for the cognitive and affective benefits of group learning for each individual learner. Second, whether or not the role of expert is filled by the teacher, or this expert is interacting with a group or an individual student, the mode of interaction is that which has been found to be characteristic of talk between young children and their parents about a topic of mutual interest (Wells 1986). The adult's stance in this sort of talk is one of "contingent responsiveness," as he or she first listens to discover the child's topic and purpose, and then makes a contribution that will enable the child to extend and develop it.

On many occasions, however, such as when a topic is being addressed through group inquiry, the teacher will not be a participant. In such situations, collaborative interaction will occur among a group of students who may be of relatively equal expertise and the role of expert will be distributed, with first one student and then another contributing on the basis of personal experience or of the information she or he has acquired. This brings us to another consequential characteristic within the collaborative mode: the different kinds of learning that are being provided regardless of the presence of a teacher in the interacting group.

In chapter 3, we contrasted the collaborative talk that occurs in these latter two contexts in terms of the different contribution that each is likely to make to students' learning. Collaborative talk between peers, we suggested, *enables* one or more of the participants to complete a task as successfully as possible. This task may be practical, such as making a model, or intellectual, such as understanding a phenomenon or composing a written document. Such talk undoubtedly provides many opportunities for learning, as well as enabling progress to be made with the task in hand. Yet, it would be naive to believe that the kinds of learning that are typically being provided for through peer collaboration, especially among children, would be the same as when an intentional teacher is present. For example, it is unlikely that peers would be explicitly concerned with facilitating the deliberate monitoring and articulation of the processes through which learning of content knowledge occurs or through which an assignment gets completed.

Where the collaborative talk is between teacher and individual learner, on the other hand, there is potential for these important benefits to occur, as we stated in chapter 3 (p. 58–60). To engage with students in this sort of contingently responsive "tutorial" talk, we believe, is one of the teacher's most important responsibilities. In fact, one might say it is the very essence of teaching. However, it is also important that teachers, in their practice, are sensitive to the distinctions discussed so far, and assume responsibility for ensuring that learners experience all the various forms of collaborative interaction so that they may fully benefit from their potential.

Finally, it is essential to recognize that there exists another form of interaction that should be treated as having equal importance for learning—interaction with oneself. Briefly stated, this form of interaction occurs when we reflect on our own understanding—when we think, as it were, through dialogue with an "internalized other" (Mead 1934) in the form of inner speech or, for example, when writing, as we alternate between the roles of reflective writer and reflective reader. Besides creating a classroom climate that is conducive to collaborative interaction, therefore, it is equally essential to ensure that there is intellectual space for meaningful individual reading and writing within a school day. The intellectual space required, however, is not merely a time provision to read and write on one's own. It should include attention to mechanisms within and beyond group-learning contexts, which provide for individual expression and development of scholarship and intellectual interests, without these interests necessarily having to be constantly subordinated to group agenda and negotiations. In classrooms where teachers are guided by this consideration, there are minimal problems of group dynamics and learners find collaborative learning satisfying and beneficial rather than frustrating, as the movement between collaborative and individual learning is fluid but well integrated.

We are suggesting, then, that there are three modes of interaction that should be provided for in the classroom in addition to the teacher's exposition. The first mode is the sharing of understanding—and ignorance—among learners, and between learners and experts, in order that they may mutually support and act as catalysts to each other in their knowing and coming to know. The second mode is tutorial talk, in which individual students benefit from expert guidance that is responsive to their particular needs. The third mode involves the provision of opportunities for students to reflect and commune with themselves through inner speech, reading, and writing. As educators, we have to strike a conscious and thoughtful balance among all three modes, because overemphasizing one may cause a stifling of the benefits of another. To strike this balance we have to take a very sensitive view of what it means to learn through interaction and realize the pitfalls associated with the common practice of defining interactive learning too narrowly. It is only by going beyond a narrow and panacea-like definition of interactive learning that we can make it a means for effective learning instead of simply something that ought to be done.

Literacy and Learning in School

Having discussed the first two principles at some length, we now wish to integrate them with our third principle, that of the centrality of literacy in intellectual development, the arguments for which have already been set forth in earlier chapters. Our aim is to present a rationale for the transformation of classrooms and schools into communities of literate thinkers.

As we said earlier, we concur with the majority of educators in considering the systematic construction of knowledge to be the major aim of education. This, we have argued, will best be achieved when it is recognized that knowledge has to be constructed by individual students through the progressive extending and modifying of their existing knowledge that occurs when they attempt to make sense of new information and experience.

This process goes on spontaneously simply as a result of encountering new experiences, but in a piecemeal and largely unconscious fashion. The function of schooling, however, is to bring the individual's knowledge, and also the processes by which it is acquired, under conscious monitoring, so that she or he may take active and intentional control over her or his own learning and be able to make connections between knowledge acquired in school and that which is acquired in practical life situations outside the classroom (Barnes 1976). For the ultimate test of what is learned is the learner's ability to exploit that knowledge to formulate and solve new problems of a practical as well as an academic nature.

Literacy, understood as the conscious exploitation of the symbolic potential of language as an instrument for thinking, provides the means for achieving this intentional control over learning. As already suggested, careful attention to a text, in order to decide what interpretations are warranted, leads to the development of a critical and reflective attitude to the linguistic formulations in which knowledge is couched; it also encourages the development of the ability to engage in thinking that is disembedded from particular concrete situations (Donaldson 1978). Writing is potentially still more powerful in requiring one to confront what one knows and does not know, and to make warranted connections as one attempts to orchestrate one's knowledge, and from that orchestration, compose a coherent text that will effectively communicate what one knows and feels. In addition, when writing involves rewriting, it provides occasions for the development of thinking about one's thinking.

But, as already argued, these skills of literate thinking can be acquired in speech as well as in reading and writing if the participants have a clear end in view that demands that they attempt to express their point of view explicitly and with due attention to the justification of their opinions (see chapter 3). Furthermore, when working on a written text, as reader or writer, there is much to be gained from talking to other people — engaging in what above we called collaborative talk for the calibration of interpretations of the written text.

Our conclusion, therefore, is that to achieve most effectively the educational goal of knowledge construction, schools and classrooms need to become communities of literate thinkers engaged in collaborative inquiries.

Inquiry in One Classroom

Having elaborated on the principles underlying our belief in the value of collaborative inquiry and literacy, let us now look at some episodes from the unit on animals in Maher's grade four class to see what are the literate consequences of an attempt to work out these principles in practice through the creation of a classroom community of active and literate learners. We will start with an episode that occurred during the first phase, that of observing a living creature.

There were several reasons for the choice of animals as the topic for this unit of study. How people and animals — and living things in general — get along in the world is a subject that Maher believes to be of central importance. Earlier in the year, the class had observed the metamorphosis of caterpillars into butterflies and, in the previous year, some of the children in the class had been involved in the study of newly hatched chicks (see chapter 1). On the present occasion, however, there was a choice of living creatures to study and so there was an opportunity for individual children to develop expertise that they could share with others who had studied a different animal.

Much of the research that the children carried out was library-based, since they consulted reference books, naturalist's guides, and other printed and illustrated material. But an important part of the project involved firsthand observation. Maher wanted the children to have the opportunity to use all their senses — touching, smelling, looking at, and listening to a particular creature, as well as reading about it. So she assembled a collection that included a crayfish, some crickets, a Mexican land crab, and a rat, as well as the guinea pig and gerbil that were regular members of the classroom community. The collection also included a colony of mealy worms. For the children to share the responsibility for looking after these creatures was a further objective of this project.

The first task was to spend some time each day observing one of these creatures either in groups or individually, and to enter the results of these observations in a log. The children were left free to select what in particular they would attend to, but to get them started Maher had them spend the first morning in self-selected groups finding out as much as they could about one of a number of key terms such as "food-chain", "ecology", and "conservation". Then, because she wanted them to interact with children with whom they did not typically choose to work, and also to avoid the wide variation in group size that might have resulted from a free choice, she got the children to draw lots to determine which creature they would observe.

Observing the Mealy Worms

Margarida drew the mealy worms and, as her first entry in her log makes clear (p. 92), her initial reaction was one of disgust. By the time she was observed in her group on the second day of the project, however, she had begun to feel differently. In the following extract, Margarida, Barbara, and Pauline have a tray of mealy worms. Margarida has put one in a small plastic beaker and is examining it intently.

1 **M**: Look how it's moving its head and crawling

2   Look look . and over there it doesn't move hardly nothing

3 **B**: Maybe it doesn't like it <u>there</u>
     (Linh, a Chinese girl, is walking by and stops to look)

4 **L**: <u>Could you</u> tell me something what you're doing

5 **B**: We're helping each other — and thinking and observing

6 **M**: Maybe if we put some more — one more in maybe it will be a little bit happier

7 **B**: Yeah put one more in

8   Look at all the other ones that are dying
       (Chung is passing. He stops to look)

9 **C**: You're not scared to pick it up?

10 **M&B**: No

11 **M**: Look how it's curling all over each other and making a shape of a P
         (Barbara looks)

12 **M**: I wonder how they die

13 **B**: I guess . they're not happy and they die

14 **M**: No

15 **B**: Why don't — why don't we go ask Mrs Maher why this one died?

16 **M**: No

17 **P**: One just went out of its shell

18 **B**: They don't have shells

19 **M**: Yes they do

20   Why are they going out of their shells?

21 **B**: They want to die?

22 **P**: No they're losing the skin

23 **M**: Yes probably — like caterpillars
         (Several boys, including Chung, stop to look)

24 **M**: They like each other

25 **C**: They don't even look like they have any legs

26 **M&B**: They DO

27 **M**: Watch (tipping the mealy worm out of the beaker and on to her
         hand)

28 **C**: They all look so ugly

29 **M**: See they have feet

30   Oh my god they all have feet on top of their head

31 **B**: They have feet on top of their head?

32 **M**: Yeah look . they're walking on it

33 **B**: I'm going to call Mrs Maher

Watching this group at work, the strongest impression is of the
intensity of their involvement, as they observe, react to, and speculate
about the apparently dying mealy worms. Even the ringing of the
bell for recess, which occurs at this point, does not interrupt their
concentration, and it is several minutes before the teacher is finally
able to persuade them to break off to go out to play. As soon as they
return, they pick up the discussion as if there had been no interrup-
tion. The next extract starts a few minutes after they have resumed
work.

46 M: But out of a hundred let's see how many are alive

47 P: Are there a hundred?

48 M: Yes

49 B: Some of them are dying

50 M: See those black stuff they're die — they're dead
(Tomas stops to look)

51 T: You picking all of them up?

52 M: They do — we have to see how they kill each other — if they kill each other or what they do

53 B: Yeah

54 T: That one's dead

55 M: No it isn't

56 B: (to Pauline) Can I take some . I never did this before I'm kind of scared

57 M: It's not dead Tomas it just moved . but it's getting dead

58   Let's watch this one first cos it's dying

59 B: (to Margarida) OK pick up this one right there
(Barbara and Pauline show some reluctance to touch the mealy worms)

60 B: This one he's dying .. You can even see he's got the black spot

61   Call Gordon I want to show him it
(Gordon joins them)

62 M: This one's — this one is starting to die because the other ones are black and he's starting to get black

63 B: Look they — they're all black

64 G: Why are those ones black?

65 M&B: Cos they're dead

66 M: And this one's starting to get black as well because it's starting to die

67 G: D'you think they go black before they die or after?

68 M: I think that's how they die

69 G: How long have you been observing them? How many days?

70 B: Um — this is our first day

71 G: OK Now have you thought how you could — you could observe the same one each day?

72 M: Well —

73 G: Is there a way you could know which ones you were looking at?

74 B: Put them in a cup

75 P: Yes that's what I said

76 M: See they're crawly

77 G: Perhaps you could think about that because if you don't know that you're looking at the same one each time you won't know how —

78 M: (to Gordon) We could put one — these ones that we're looking at in a cup . for a day **** or we could — (turning to Pauline as Gordon moves away)

79   Because these are the ones we're watching

80   We want to watch them every day to see how they're growing

81 P: Look at this one

82 M: I know . isn't it AMAZING!

Two aspects seem worth singling out for attention. The first is the way in which observation leads to speculation and the beginnings of more systematic inquiry. On a number of occasions (e.g., lines 17, 25, and 54) an observation by one child sets off a disagreement, which leads to a more careful observation by all of them. For example, Chung's comment that they do not appear to have any legs (23) leads to Margarida's discovery that they have "feet on top of their head" (29 — 30). Or, more significantly for the understanding that they eventually achieve, Pauline's observation that "one just went out of its shell" (17) is countered by Margarida's assertion that they do not have shells; this in turn leads Pauline to look again and observe that it is a skin that is being shed and this reminds Margarida of the caterpillars they had studied earlier in the year (23). At this stage, the girls are working on the hypothesis (discovered later to be erroneous) that the dark-colored worms are dead, and much of their speculation is concerned with the supposed processes and causes of death (58 — 68). Quite early on, Pauline suggests that they separate them into two groups and, following Gordon's prompting, this becomes the basis for Margarida's more systematic proposal (79 — 80) to separate them "because these are the ones we're watching. We want to watch them every day to see how they're growing."

The spirit in which the children build upon each other's speculations about the changing colors of their mealy worms is quite remarkable. Their observations and interest in extending their understanding are so intimately linked that they generate a spontaneity to utilize their projection abilities, focusing upon making meaning of an observable phenomenon rather than arguing about the factual accuracy of each other's contributions. If the latter had occurred, it could easily have led to issues of group dynamics — which are noticeably absent among the children. The exchanges between Margarida and her friends demonstrate that to achieve a classroom climate that disposes children to engage in literate behavior, one must understand more than the learning activities that contribute to it. One must understand how the teacher's goals, collaborative interactions, and the classroom as a whole come together to create a curriculum of opportunities for literacy development.

The second notable aspect is the affective tone to so much of the talk. There seem to be two sources. First, the apparent sickly state of the worms arouses their concern—"I guess they're not happy and they die" (13), and "Maybe if we put one more in maybe it will be a little bit happier" (6). The anthropomorphic attribution of affective states to other living creatures, even mealy worms, seems to be a natural response of children of this age. The second source is to be found in their own conflicting reactions to these creatures. The initial reaction, strongly expressed in Margarida's journal entry, is one of disgust; but this is counterpointed by the empathy already referred to and by the fascination that is aroused by the close observation of any living creature. The latter wins out, as is clear from their desire to share their observations with the adults in the room and from Margarida's last comment, "Isn't it AMAZING!"

Margarida's group was by no means unique; the same sort of involvement was to be seen in all the other groups. We have quoted this episode at length because, at first sight, mealy worms might seem unlikely to arouse such a response. Too often, when we are selecting curriculum topics, we consider them only in terms of their cognitive content or the skill learning they promote. These are important matters, of course, but they ignore the affective dimension. Our observation of Margarida and her friends reminded us how important this is in providing the energy that enables children to become absorbed in a topic and to stay on task for extended periods of time. Once we had been alerted to this dimension of their activities, we began to notice how the children's expression of their feelings about the topics they were working on acted like the warp on which the more cognitive weft was woven in all the discourses they were creating in speech and writing.

Here are two more examples, taken from Kathryn's journal, entitled "The Newt Study":

Tues. Jan 12, 88.

The newt only goes up when nobody is looking at it. The newt never realy pays attention to the guppies. When the newt goes up he wiggedes up. When he moves he really moves but when he stayes still he's like a statuw. The newt dosen't like to be watched but when he is he dosen't care. We feed shrimp to eat. The newt likes to stay at corner at the bottom of the aquarium. He also likes going throgh rocks witch is daingres because the crayfish is there. We put the basket in to see how the newt would react. It looks like the newt is smelling the basket. Soon it claimed [climbed] on the basket and started swimming up to the top then suddenly swam to the bottom of the aquarium.

Thurs. Jan 14, 88.

Today a very sad thing happened in our class. Wendy found the newt in the molded pumpkin box. It was very dry. And another thing. . . . It was dead. We decided to leave it there for now. We hadn't even thought up a name for it. Mani, Janice and I felt like crying. He was just getting use to being held too. It had allredy loved to be peted. I'll miss him.

There is no doubt about Kathryn's involvement with the newt, or about the sense of loss that she feels at the death of this little creature that she was getting to know through careful observation and through the sense of touch: "We hadn't even thought up a name for it." At the same time, in communicating her response to the event, she is clearly also intent on creating a dramatic effect for her audience in the way she delays the revelation of the nature of the "very sad thing that happened." At first, the details of where and how the newt was found do not seem to merit the gravity of her characterization of the event and this effect is further reinforced by the way in which she appears to be introducing another detail of the same kind. However, the four periods that follow create a sudden feeling of anticipation — all the greater for having been preceded by the disarming "And another thing" — so that when the truth is finally revealed a much stronger effect is produced than would have been the case if it had been announced in the first sentence.

Kathryn's journal, like those of many of her classmates, is a window onto the child's observational abilities, among other skills. But more significantly, it is primarily a forum within which she, the learner, can explore her observations in detail and with involved projection as she reobserves the newt through writing. The journal thus affords, within the collaborative activity of adopting a living animal to study, an opportunity for individual exploration of various personal meanings and emergent learning goals by each learner. And, in the case of Kathryn at this stage of her observations, it is her interest in the newt's behavior in response to its environment and other creatures around it. Thus, it is of little surprise that the following day Kathryn's writing expresses her strong sense of loss at its death at a time when she was just beginning to discover that "He was just geting use to being held too. It had allredy loved to be peted." Indeed, the keeping of a journal is a practice that encourages children to utilize their literate skills to discover what they are enthusiastic about, and from there to develop further newfound knowledge and learning interests.

Reporting on the Frog

Alongside the observation of one of the living creatures in the classroom, each child was required to research from books an animal of his or her choice, either alone or in a small group. Having selected the animal, they were asked to identify a question to give focus to their research.

Kathryn had started by observing the newt with a group of friends and then gone on alone to study the frog, focusing on the frog's method of reproduction. Having completed her book research on the frog, she had prepared a display on a small table to communicate the results of her inquiry to others. This consisted of a model of a pond with male and female frogs, a written description of the frogs' method of reproduction, and a diagram of the reproductive organs of the male frog. On either side of the model were the books that she had consulted, including a naturalist's guide to North American reptiles, an illustrated book about frogs, and a book about reptiles. She also included a copy of the fairy tale, "The Frog Prince."

In the following episode, Kathryn is teaching what she has learned about the frog to three boys from her class, Lionel, Justin, and Tomas. Kathryn is standing by the table using a ruler to point to the various parts of her display. The three boys are sitting facing her. As in the previous episode, the interest of all participants is very apparent. This can be gauged both from the interactive nature of the discourse and from the fact that, throughout the twenty minutes they are observed, they never deviate from the topic. An added zest is provided by the interplay between the interpersonal relationship between the presenter (female) and audience (male) and the question she has chosen to study (reproduction).

The episode starts by Kathryn placing the frog in relation to the newt "I found this quite weird actually that they're in the same family but they're enemies," she says, and this leads to a discussion of some of the different varieties of frogs. Kathryn then turns to her own written text and begins to read from it, referring also to her accompanying diagram. In the extract that follows, she refers also to one of the reference books she had used.

28 K: Millions of sperms are stored until ejected *** so this is like the—it comes right there (pointing to her diagram)

29 L: So you are saying like this—
(Kathryn picks up the book from which she took the diagram and shows it to the three boys)

30 K: In here . the picture . here's the picture

31 T: Is this the female?

32 K: Yeah I didn't draw it (i.e., the diagram of the female)

33 T: Yeah I—I can see

34 J: Oh I get it . you see this is the picture over there . (pointing to the diagram of the male frog in the book and then to Kathryn's diagram) this is the picture over there

35 L: Yeah this is the male . and that's the female . (pointing to pictures in the book)
<u>because it needs that</u> . . it needs that for the eggs

36 K: <u>This is where</u>—this is where the eggs are stored

37 L: So this is like the pouch—the pouch and this is um—

38 T: Yeah these are eggs

39 K: But this is not the whole body (pointing to diagram) this is the * part

    Although Kathryn is the "expert," the other children do not sit back, passively absorbing the information she has to present. This is truly a social activity, as the three boys bring their knowledge to bear in understanding what she has to tell them, asking questions and offering their interpretations of each other's contributions. This is clearly an example of what we have called the co-construction of knowledge. And, in the following extract, one can see very clearly how this joint construction is enacted in the very form of the discourse.

    The sequence starts after a slight lull in the conversation which follows, and is perhaps induced by, Lionel's comparison between frogs and sharks.

54 L: So then—then . you know what I think . what's different from other animals like the shark .

55   When the shark mates it has a fight and it gets scars . but like I don't think the frog fights and gets scars

56 K: (laughs) No I don't think it—

57   But um . . .

58 L: Where—where do they go like—where do they go when um—like <u>*</u>

59 K: <u>*</u> when they—when they mate?

60 L: No . when they um—when like there's a tornado?

61 J: This is how they ⟨breed⟩?

62 K: (laughs)

63 J: Like—like—do they have—do they have a shelter?

64 K: Yeah I guess so I <u>guess they</u> just um—they go—

65 T: <u>under water</u>

66 K: Yeah they go under water when they think something's wrong and like they —

67 J: It sometimes happens . that <u>*</u>

68 L: <u>So</u> . how long do you think a frog can stay in the water?

69 K: Well . I think quite a long time because you know .

70 L: They stay under <u>water</u>

71 K: <u>Yeah</u> because they breathe when they stay under water

In line 58, perhaps through association with his previous contribution, Lionel is trying to move the discussion to another important dimension of the ecological study of the frog, namely its strategies for survival in the face of danger. As he pauses to find an appropriate term for what he has in mind, Kathryn, assuming that he is making reference to the current topic of discussion, reproduction, offers a completion to his question (59). This is not, however, what Lionel has in mind. In an attempt to make himself understood, he offers an instance of a hazard: "when like there's a tornado?" (60). Justin's next utterance (61) seems to be trying to make a connection between mating and tornados but, judging by Kathryn's laughing response and his continuation, Justin's question was probably to check his understanding of Lionel's question. His follow-up query (63), in fact, represents another attempt, and at this point everyone in the group understands Lionel. As the expert, Kathryn feels it incumbent upon her to provide an answer. However, she is clearly uncertain on this matter, until Tomas offers his suggestion (65). With Justin's and Tomas's participation, she formulates an answer that addresses Lionel's interest in frog behavior in the face of danger: "They go under water when they think something's wrong" (66). Very naturally, Lionel becomes curious about how long frogs can remain underwater, if that is the way they cope with danger. Implicit in his question (68) and its extension (70), is the active meaning-making behavior that children engage in when they encounter what perhaps is dissonant or implausibe information in the light of their own knowledge or experience — their tendency to search for answers.

Our point in discussing this extract at some length is to illustrate one part of the learning process *in action*. So often, the process appears to be unidirectional: teacher or text tells, and the student is assumed to have absorbed the information. What is ignored, because it is unseen, is the internal equivalent of what is made external in the previous extract; the process of bringing existing knowledge to bear in actively construing and interpreting the information that is made available through the posing of questions and, just as important, the search for answers. Among peers, this process is made fully apparent, as the contribution of one student is extended, challenged, or modified by the contributions of the others.

Ideally, the same process should be encouraged when the teacher is one of the participants but, as has frequently been demonstrated, the inequality of status between teacher and student militates against the sort of collaborative construction of knowledge that has just been illustrated (Barnes 1969; Mehan 1979; Sinclair and Coulthard 1975). It is for this reason that we are urging that students should be given opportunities to engage in small group learning; these situations encourage them to take a much more active role in making meaning than when they are expected to be relatively passive recipients of information transmitted by teacher or textbook.

However, it may be objected that, without a teacher present to monitor and direct the discussion, there is a risk that some of the information that is contributed will be inaccurate and that the knowledge that is constructed will therefore be incomplete or, worse still, false. There is indeed such a risk. But there is equally a risk that, when the information comes from teacher or textbook, the interpretation that the student puts upon it will also be inaccurate. However, this inaccuracy goes undetected unless the student has the opportunity to externalize his or her own understanding in a variety of ways, such as commenting, questioning, providing answers, or reformulating a contribution through collaborative interaction. It is these opportunities that the group situation positively encourages (Sharan and Sharan 1976). Furthermore, where the students are themselves responsible for the meaning that is jointly constructed, they are much more likely to adopt a critical stance to the suggestions that are made than in the transmission mode of learning, in which information from teacher or text is accepted uncritically because it comes with the stamp of the expert's authority (Olson 1980).

As was emphasized earlier in the chapter, the group learning situation is not only a natural but also a catalystic means of learning. Nevertheless, the actual construction of knowledge still remains the responsibility of the individual learner, and much of it goes on as unobservable tacit internal operations of the mind. It is for this reason that the externalizing or making public of students' thinking on a topic of inquiry needs to be encouraged. However, besides the oral mode, a written outcome of some kind should form an integral component of any group learning situation. Because of the more stringent demands for explicitness and systematicity of exposition that are placed on a writer by the anticipated needs of the audience, writing provides the learner with an individualized opportunity to confront his or her own knowledge, and to learn to develop a self-conscious stance towards the completeness and coherence of his or her understanding. It is in this dialectical interplay between what Scardamalia and Bereiter (1985) refer to as the "rhetorical space" and the "problem space" that writing develops an individual's thinking and knowledge.

Thus, as the boys together read Kathryn's text on the frog's reproductive system and, at the same time, listen to her presentation, the children as a group utilize writing in this dialectical manner.

> The femal frog can make as many as 2000 eggs inside its body. To make a egg into a tadpole and then into a frog is very difficult. The eggs have to go into alot of different tubes and passways in the mothers body befor they are ready to get out. The femal frog is fat and heavy while carring the eggs. This slowes it down and makes it hard to escape from its enamys. To make a frog one egg of the femal must first be fertilized by the sperm of a male frog. The male makes millions of sperm in testes. They pass to the kidneys though the sperm ducts into the sperm sac. Where millions of sperm are stored untill ejected through the cloaca.

At this point, Kathryn's written account represents what she knows. But it is noticeable that, as she makes her presentation and the three boys actively listen to her, the group naturally uses her written account as the fulcrum upon which they compare their understanding and the adequacy of Kathryn's composition of what she knows. And, in so doing — as the ensuing discussion among the children demonstrates — she has the opportunity to discover the limitations both of her knowledge and of the way in which she has presented it to her audience. Clearly, Kathryn's somewhat clinical account has failed to answer what is for Justin a really important point about reproduction.

84 J: When — when they mate — when they get on top of each other like —

85 K: No

86 J: Does — does the female get on top of the male or does the **

87 ?:   *****

88 K: They really just (laughing) go like that (demonstrating) (laughs)

89 L: I know hug each other **

90 J: But — but do they um — is the male on top of the female or the female on top of the male?

91 **K**: They don't really lie down and do it . kind of just sideways

92 **J**: Yeah I know

93 **L**: I know they sort of <u>like</u>—

94 **J**:   **

95 **K**: The male's right here right?

96   And the female goes over there and <u>he</u> . hugs her because um—

96 **J**:   <u>yeah</u>

97 **L**: He hugs her?

98 **K**: Yeah like that (demonstrating putting her arms round an imaginary body)

99 **T**: Yeah

100 **L**: He hugs her? (sounding unconvinced)

101   I thought they—

102 **K**: (laughs with embarrassment) I think ** different

103 **J**: How—how big can a frog get?

Although somewhat embarassed, Kathryn struggles to convey what she has learned, making use of gesture when words fail. On this basis, Lionel obligingly offers the term "hugs" to describe the action of the male with respect to the female. But in the end it is he who questions its appropriateness in a tone of exaggerated scepticism that is impossible to transcribe. After this collaborative construction of understanding, it would have been really worthwhile if, at this point, there had been an opportunity for Kathryn to attempt a revision of her written account of the mating habits of the frog.

For this group of children, then—as for the others in the class—literate behavior is not restricted to meaningful reading and writing, but embraces an intertextual space that includes the child's writing, books of reference, diagrams and illustrations, and the oral discussion that surrounds and interprets the various texts. If, as we have suggested, the hallmark of literate thinking is the exploitation of the symbolic potential of external representation as an aid to the construction of inner meaning, these children are clearly engaged in literate thinking as they move, through talk, between the written verbal formulation, the diagrams, and the illustration, in order to be sure that they have understood. As is so often the case, what is read needs to be reformulated in one's own words—orally or in writing—and checked against the formulations of others, in order that whatever new information is constructed from intersubjective perspectives may be integrated into one's personal knowledge.

Co-reflecting on the Processes of Inquiry

Something that was noticeable in all of the above episodes was the children's openness to new ways of thinking and feeling in the face of new questions. Although they themselves would probably not have used the term "revision", they had begun to be influenced by their teacher's growing awareness of the pervasive appropriateness of this attitude to tasks undertaken and to decisions made (see chapter 1). As when writing, the first attempt is rarely the best one can achieve; rather, it represents the struggle through the foothills of meaning making to a plateau from which a clearer view can be obtained of the goal that one is attempting to reach and of the route by which one may get to it.

Topic choice is a case in point. Choosing a topic is an essential, but often one of the most difficult, parts of undertaking any inquiry. On this occasion, the project started with a class brainstorming session in which the children were encouraged to consider which animal they would like to study and, equally important, what question in particular they wanted to try to answer. Following this initial discussion, they were asked, when they had reached a decision, to sign up on the topic board with their topic and question. However, it was also made clear that it was quite acceptable for them subsequently to change their topic or question, provided that they recorded the change. The teacher regularly monitored the entries on the board and used them as a basis for conferences with individuals and groups about their topic choices.

The following is the transcript of one such conference. The teacher has gathered a group of children around the topic board and, having noticed that Justin has changed his mind about his topic, she invites him to talk about the reasons for his decision.

1 T: Justin . You've changed your mind a couple of times

2 J: Yes

3 T: D'you think you could talk about why you changed your mind?

4 J: Well I dunno . The catfish it just kinda sat there

5 T: (laughs)

6 J: The catfish wasn't that exciting and the jellyfish um — like I couldn't find much books about the jellyfish and it just didn't —

7 T: Fine . So I see you've got lion down here

8   You were talking on Friday — I know from your African . experiences . so you might be a little familiar

9 J: Yes I did it because um — I — I er — already know something about it

10 T: And have you remembered that most important part about "You must be interested in what you're doing" (This had been discussed in the earlier brainstorming session about choosing a topic/question for a project and was written on the blackboard)

11 J: Yes I know

12 T: You are . . You haven't got a question here yet . . .

13   Have you thought about a question in your mind about the lion?

14 J: Yes

15 T: Are you able to talk about that yet?

16 J: Well I haven't really got one yet

17 T: You're still thinking, OK.

18   While we're talking this morning in this little group for a few minutes . listen to what other people say .

19   You'll probably get some good ideas

The teacher then turns to some of the other children to listen to their accounts and to ask about their progress. Seth has decided to try to discover how fishes move and, after considering some possible avenues for exploration, the teacher says "We'll all be really keen on hearing what you find out Seth." Sarah plans to do her research on rabbits — where they live and what they eat. Wendy also wants to study rabbits — "What they like to eat. What they eat in the wild," to which, after accepting the proposal, the teacher replies "It would be interesting to see if you have to make that question bigger to keep yourself interested." Sarah and Wendy decide to work together and, interestingly, they do indeed expand their question to a study of the similarities and differences between members of the rodent family. The final outcome of their inquiry was a well-researched and attractively presented display entitled "Rodentland."

As the teacher discovered, the topic board became a point of reference both for her and for the children. Frequently, a small group could be seen looking at the choices made by other children and changes in topic were noticed and remarked on; they also saw that the teacher made frequent reference to the entries on the board to help her in her planning, and that she, too, was interested in the reasons for the changes that were made. In this way, the acceptability of revising goals and plans was given implicit recognition and explicitly brought to conscious attention through writing as well as group discussion. The jottings on the topic board thus constituted a visible trace of the teacher's and children's co-determination of the topic questions raised for consideration. More importantly, they formed a common text, around which justifications, planning, and reflections on the actions taken or not taken in the course of the children's inquiry were conducted. Indeed, the topic board served to make a very tangible and concrete link between each child's learning at any one point in time and her or his past decisions and future actions, thereby enabling the child to engage with the teacher in reflection about the processes through which her or his inquiry moved.

The next example concerns an even more direct consideration of some of the processes involved in carrying out an inquiry, and it involved the whole class. At the beginning of the project, the teacher had asked the children to think about the sorts of learning the project might lead them to engage in and they had come up with a list that included the following:

observing
reading
writing about
thinking about
talking about
asking questions
experimenting
making models
creating

Subsequently, at Lionel's suggestion, this list became the basis for a tracking sheet, a copy of which each child filled in at the end of each day, as a record of what he or she had been doing.

At the end of the project, in reviewing with the class what they had achieved and the sorts of activities in which they had engaged, the teacher invited the children to reconsider their original list of types of learning. For twenty minutes or so, the children worked in self-chosen groups, evaluating the categories on the list in the light of their experience, with a view to possible revisions. When the whole class regathered, there was further discussion of the reports from the various groups. In the end, one change was made to the list as a result of a suggestion from Lionel who proposed the addition of "feeling," in the sense of learning by touching. (Despite instructions to the contrary, Lionel had picked up and examined the Mexican land crab.)

However, as argued earlier, the value of the revision process does not lie only in the changes that may be made, but also in the qualitative changes in understanding that may result from a focused scrutiny of the current text in order to discover what it means, and to evaluate its internal coherence and its adequacy as a representation of the author's intention. Another important reason for the teacher's inclusion of the review of the tracking sheet within the total collaborative inquiry on animals had been to provide the children with opportunities to learn from reseeing their learning processes. This is as important as the learning that arises from reseeing products as the outcomes of engaging in those processes. But, all too often, this is neglected or overlooked. We believe it is an extremely important aspect of the curriculum if children are to develop their strategic knowledge and become autonomous learners.

The following extract from a discussion between Kathryn and her two friends, Mani and Janice, demonstrates the value of providing such opportunities. It comes from the recording that was made while the children were engaged in their small groups in their attempt to resee the list of intellectual processes in which they had been involved as they carried out their inquiries on animals.

1 **M**: But 'created'

2 **J**: 'Created' I don't really get that

3 **M**: Do you know what 'created' means?

4 **K**: Yeah . you made it . like er —

5 **J**: Then that's just like you made models (referring to the previous category)

6 **K**: I created an idea (trying out the collocation)

7   You can say it with ideas but you can't model an idea

8   Like you can model things . but creating —

9 **J**: Yeah but if you have an idea about —

10 **K**:   Creating a thought

11 **J**: But if you have an idea of —

12 **K**: Like creating a story

13 **J**: But if you have an idea of a lion . you can model a lion

14   So that's part of the thing

15 **K**: Yeah so 'created' also means 'model' . almost the same thing

As they engage in co-reflection to revise the tracking sheet, these three girls find themselves being challenged to test their understanding of the terms "creating" and "making models," and they attempt to clarify the relationship between them by relating the words to the particular activities in which they and their friends had been engaging. Through grappling in this way with the subtle conceptual distinctions coded in language, they are led, in turn, to reflect upon their recent experiences from a metacognitive perspective — a perspective that is rarely adopted in the course of actually completing a learning task.

A Model for an Inquiry-based, Writing-oriented Curriculum

In presenting and analyzing these episodes selected from one specific classroom project, we have tried to illustrate the quality of the intellectual life that can occur in a classroom that functions as a community of literate thinkers. We have also tried to show how such a community is created both by establishing between all participants working relationships that are collaborative rather than directive or competitive, and by organizing the structure of the overall task in such a manner that exposition, group work, and individual endeavor are integrated in goal-oriented and meaningful ways. As we have argued throughout this chapter, people learn most successfully when they have the freedom to make choices about the activities in which they engage and are given support, through processes of co-determination, of what to learn, and how best to do so. At the same time, for all of us — children, teachers, and researchers — the construction of knowledge requires goal-directed engagement with new information, through direct experience and exposition, through discussion and deliberation with others, and through communing with self in writing and reading.

Although less explicitly, we have also tried, in the preceding pages, to communicate something of the intellectual life that went on beyond the classroom as we, the authors, collaborated with each other in our study of literacy and learning in the classroom, thereby forming another learning community. In doing so, we have made frequent use of analogies from writing. This is not accidental. Both as experienced teachers and as practicing researchers, we have drawn on our knowledge of what enables writers in order to inform our thinking about what enables learning through inquiry. From our recognition of the connections between these two activities, seen in the work described in this chapter, as well as that reported in the chapter that follows, we gradually developed a model for conceptualizing an inquiry-centered curriculum, which is shown diagrammatically in figure 5−1.

Such a curriculum would be organized in terms of broad thematic units of study, such as living creatures, which provide a framework within which individual students or small groups negotiate particular topics for investigation with their teacher according to their personal interests, the feasibility of the suggested topic, and the resources available. At the end of the unit of study, individual or group projects are presented to the rest of the class and perhaps also to other classes in the school; in some cases they may also be presented at an open house or on a parents' evening. As in chapter 3

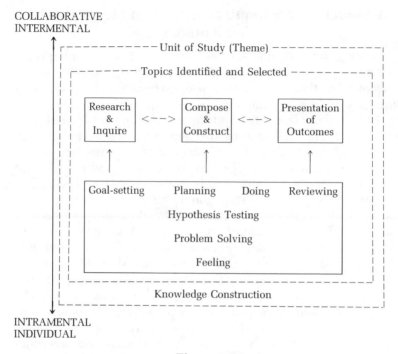

Figure 5−1
Model of an Inquiry-centered Curriculum.

and the present case, the unit will probably start with some whole class activity, in which the students explore what they already know about the topic and brainstorm possible questions to investigate. Throughout the unit, too, the overall theme provides a context for the individual inquiries and enables links to be drawn between them. Finally, in a concluding whole-class discussion, the work of the different groups is reviewed in order to consolidate the understandings that have been achieved, to identify further questions for future investigation, and to reflect on the procedures and strategies that have proved effective in the various phases of the inquiries that have been carried out.

It is at this level of procedures and strategies that the connections between inquiring and writing are most apparent. Both types of activity involve three major components, which we have labeled research and inquire, compose and construct, and presentation of outcomes. Whether in writing or in conducting an inquiry, there is a necessary component of collecting information relevant to the topic through reading, observation, experimentation, and so on. The information collected must then be assembled, organized and interpreted in order to make sense of it — to discover what meaning it has for oneself. In the third component, the interests and needs of the audience come to the fore, as one works on the personal meaning one has constructed in order to shape it into a form in which it can be effectively shared with others. These three components may be tackled sequentially; however, it is more probable that they will interact with each other in a cyclical fashion as the project as a whole develops towards the final "text" to be presented. Whatever the temporal relationship between them, all three components of an inquiry will involve, as in writing, the same essential processes of goal setting, planning, doing, and reviewing, with the latter process leading, where necessary, to revisions to what has been done, to the plans for doing, or even to the goals of the activity itself.

As we have tried to show in the diagram, the processes involved in carrying out an inquiry and in writing call upon a range of skills of hypothesis testing and problem solving. These may already form part of the learner's existing repertoire. However, as was seen in the present unit of work, some students found themselves needing to develop new skills, and many became more aware of skills that they were already using. This was brought out particularly in the initial consideration of the types of learning that the children thought they might be engaging in and in the final review of the tracking sheet, in which their initial ideas were given expression. Most importantly, underpinning both processes and skills, is what we have here called feeling — the affective involvement that provides the driving force for engagement in the activity as a whole. Finally, as is indicated on the left side of the diagram, the construction of knowledge that takes place through both inquiry and writing involves the full gamut of types of interaction, from collaborative talk with peers and teacher to individual communing with self, as the resources of the culture are first encountered in *inter*mental social activity and then gradually appropriated and transformed into a personal *intra*mental resource.

Conclusion

During the present project on animals and in the writing that has emerged from it, the applicability of our model has been further explored and refined, both by the researchers and, simultaneously, by the children, as their attention was implicitly and explicitly drawn to the intellectual processes they were engaging in as they pursued their inquiries. For all of us, the analogy between writing and inquiry has proved illuminating.

However, in concluding this chapter, we should like to make one further point by drawing the attention of the reader to the cultural and linguistic heritages of the children in this classroom. These included members of Portuguese, Chinese, Vietnamese, Indian, and Caribbean groups, among others. Indeed, almost all the children were learning English as their second or third language or dialect. The message is therefore clear. Whether in monolingual or multilingual classrooms, equal outcomes for all children can best be maximized, regardless of cultural and linguistic background, by providing collaborative learning opportunities that integrate a wide range of uses of oral and written language with action and reflection. For the success with which children engage in literate thinking depends first and foremost on the opportunities they are given to use whatever linguistic resources they have in order to come to know and to communicate their understanding to others. Where learning is conceptualized in this way, children develop their thinking *and* their language together.

Chapter Six

Concepts of Literacy and Their Consequences for Children's Potential as Learners

During the last twenty years or so, the traditional conception of literacy as simply the possession of the skills necessary for an individual to encode or decode a written text has been transformed in a number of important ways. First, it is no longer possible to make a sharp distinction between spoken and written language simply on the basis of the mode of language used. Research comparing spoken and written texts produced by the same individuals in a variety of situations (Chafe 1985) makes it clear that there are indeed certain differences between texts that result from their means of production. However, when the same texts are compared with respect to such important dimensions as the degree to which meaning is made explicit or the author's personal involvement is made apparent in the message, it is clear that texts vary more according to their intended purpose and audience than according to whether they are spoken or written. As a result, it has been recognized that literacy is better seen as a way of using language for particular intellectual and communicative purposes than as just any use of the written mode. From this, it is a short step to the recognition that the beginnings of literacy occur in the pre-school years in the child's oral participation in shared literacy events before he or she can read or write for him or herself (Heath 1986), and that the achievement of literacy requires much more than the mastery of the skills of decoding and encoding.

Second, although the actual acts of reading and writing, like those of speaking and listening, are necessarily individual, the contexts in which such acts occur is always essentially social, as are the purposes that texts are designed to serve. Texts are written to be read by a reader, even if, in some cases such as shopping lists or diaries, that reader is the writer in a different place or time. They are also written with an interpersonal purpose, whether it be to inform, persuade, direct, or delight; also they anticipate some response or reaction from the person or persons to whom they are directed. Furthermore, they are written against a background of other texts, and are most fully understood when knowledge of this background can be brought to bear in their creation as well as their interpretation. Genres such as novels, newspaper editorials, car maintenance manuals, and so on, are recognizable as such quite largely because they exploit ways of using language that have developed to meet particular purposes within a literate community and their effectiveness depends, to a considerable extent, on familiarity with those conventions. In many cases, too, the writing or reading of a text also involves a considerable amount of speech, as one seeks someone with whom to discuss the significance of what one has read or a sympathetic reader to comment on what one has written.

Third, as the processes of reading and writing have been studied in their contexts of use, it has been recognized that, far from merely providing a means for giving a permanent visual representation to speech, the written text—and the processes of composition that it entails—constitute a technology that can significantly enhance mental capacity. By making a record of thought available for reflection and, if necessary, revision, a written text serves as a "cognitive amplifier" (Bruner 1972), allowing the reader or writer to bootstrap his or her own thinking in a more powerful and intentional manner than is normally possible in speech.

From an educational perspective, then, what is important about literacy is not so much the specific information that is gained through engaging in the activities of reading and writing—important though it is—as it is the development of what, in the previous chapter, was termed literate thinking: the building up, metaphorically speaking, of a set of mental muscles that enable one effectively to tackle intellectual tasks that would otherwise be beyond one's powers.

By focusing on literate thinking in this way, and in particular on the role of writing as a tool for thinking, we intend to draw attention to the centrality of literacy in education; but not literacy conceived simply in terms of the skills of handling the conventions of the written code or those involved in the transmission of information through written texts. What we are emphasizing, rather, is a conception of literacy as a mode of thinking that deliberately makes use of language, whether spoken or written, as an instrument for its own development.

If this general line of argument is correct, there are very substantial implications for the way in which the teaching and learning of literacy should be approached in school, and indeed, there are similar implications for the curriculum as a whole. However, as our observational research study showed, these ways of thinking are, as yet, largely unknown to many teachers and so they have little impact on classroom practice. In the place of this broad and powerful conception of literacy as both means and model for creative and critical thinking, the conception underlying much actual classroom practice is both restricted and restricting. One of the aims of the Language and Learning Project, therefore, was to bring about a closer relationship between theory and practice by working collaboratively with teachers to reflect on current practice with a view to improving children's opportunities for learning. This chapter is based on work carried out with two teachers in one of the four participating schools.

The Two Classrooms Observed

Grade five, located in room 130, was a place in which all twenty-six children moved around freely and spoke to each other as much as to their teacher, whom we shall call Mr. Michael Dougherty. He believes firmly in books as a rich source of language input and, throughout the fall and spring terms, he devoted a substantial portion of each day to reading to and with the children. In language arts periods, children either worked individually or in small groups according to ability levels or commonality of interests; at other times, children worked on teacher-directed tasks, such as a series of problems in mathematics, or following guided steps, using the kits of materials provided, in science. Yet it was not unusual for the grade five children to postpone or altogether forget about doing the work set, since Michael Dougherty was extremely lenient about checking the children's work. Indeed, his trusting attitude with respect to the monitoring of work to be done was often perceived by the children as a lack of clear expectations.

In room 301, where the grade three class was located, Mrs. Margaret Thomson had developed a close relationship with her twenty-two children. Besides being expected to work individually at their desks, for example, on language and mathematic skill-related activities, the children also had opportunities to work in groups on theme-oriented activities. Often these group activities, which integrated language with curricular content, appeared to be treated as a bonus, because the children were encouraged to engage in them only after completing their daily seatwork. While the children worked alone or in groups, Thomson would frequently instruct individual children on a particular set of skills or grammatical point. She also regularly checked the children's work and kept a detailed record of the work completed by each child.

In both classrooms, we observed that reading and writing were predominantly treated as skills that required the allocation of specific times for their learning. In reading periods, it was not unusual to observe the children in both classes grouped according to reading level, reading the group reader, and completing the accompanying exercises. Similarly, in writing periods, children wrote in folders or journals about their personal experiences or on story topics that were either selected by the writer or suggested by the teacher. When the topic was teacher-selected, there would usually be a period of oral preparation, in which elements to be included in the story would be discussed (grade three) or ways of generating possible content suggested (grade five). During the actual writing, there was little teacher intervention, although there was much discussion among peers. In neither class did we observe regular opportunities for children to share what they had written with their peers, nor were the teachers observed to devote a significant amount of time to the discussion of first drafts with their authors.

The major difference between the two classes was in the amount of teacher-directed practice of skills. In grade three, a substantial proportion of the reading period (25 percent) was devoted to phonics and grammar exercises; in addition, a separate period was devoted to work on spelling and handwriting. At no time was a child seen to engage in sustained reading of a book of his or her own choice. In grade five, by contrast, much less time was spent on individual skill-based seatwork (6 percent); instead, children spent approximately one-fifth of their time engaged in silent reading of books of their own choice. In both classes, these periods allocated to the learning of reading and writing, although spent differently, accounted for approximately 45 percent of curricular time. Some time (approximately 10 to 20 percent according to our observations) was devoted to work in science and social studies. Most of this time was spent on whole-class discussion or on the completion of teacher-structured tasks (grade three) or on teacher-defined practical activities (grade five).

From such methods of classroom organization, we inferred that both teachers conceived of writing and reading primarily as language skills to be mastered as ends in themselves. Athough they differed somewhat in the means they employed to achieve these results, neither teacher seemed to encourage active discussion of alternative interpretations of the texts that the groups read together, nor did they seem to demonstrate to the children that writing could be a way of coming to know and of communicating that knowledge to others.

The Problem: Teachers' and Researchers' Perspectives

By the middle of the school year, both teachers had become sufficiently accustomed to the presence of researchers in their classrooms for the observations to be no longer perceived as threatening, and a relationship of mutual trust was beginning to be established. Informal discussions began to take place in recess time and at the end of the school day, in which the teachers began to talk about their concerns. In both cases, the poor quality of the children's writing was a topic that was frequently raised. Since writing activities constituted a considerable proportion of class time, the children's limited success as writers could not, in the teachers' views, be the result of lack of opportunity. Instead, they tended to attribute it to the children's limited command of English or to the parents' inability to give support at home, either because of the long hours that they worked, or because they were unaware of ways in which they could help, despite their concern that their children should succeed in school.

To have challenged these explanations directly would have been inappropriate. In the first place, there was some truth in the observation that the children's ability to write was affected by the fact that they were simultaneously learning the language in which they were expected to demonstrate their ability. Indeed, 86 percent of the grade three class and 92 percent of the grade five class were from non-English-speaking backgrounds. In the second place, we judged that a better approach would be to try to bring about a change in the conditions for writing by engaging in teacher-researcher collaboration such that the children's resultant behavior and performance would lead the teachers to change their opinions on the basis of empirical observations. In addition, we hypothesized that the limited potential that the children manifested in their writing was more apparent than real, and that it stemmed as much from low expectations and the nature of the challenges set for them as from any inherent limitations in the children themselves. More-over, as suggested above, an equally important constraint on the opportunities for the children to display their full potential as writers, we believed, was the teachers' underlying conception of literacy and its development.

Collaboration in Effecting Change

It is perhaps unusual to devote so much space to the description of the situation in which the researcher intends to "intervene." How-ever, we have felt it necessary to do so in order that the grounds for the intervention and the nature of the intervention itself should be understood. For, unlike those who work within what might be called the traditional paradigm of educational research and devel-opment, our intention was not to introduce an alternative curriculum package that we judged to be superior, and then measure its effec-tiveness in some way. Of course, we had principles that we thought would underpin a more effective model of literacy in the curriculum, but we also recognized that any change in that direction would need to be organic—that is to say, it would have to be chosen by the teacher and would probably be achieved incrementally over a considerable period of time.

Our reasons for adopting this approach were twofold: first, we wished to support teachers' professionalism, by inviting them to be co-agents with us in the determination of directions for change and in the means for achieving it; second, we saw the collaborative inquiry in which we were seeking to engage the teachers as itself an example of the sort of literate thinking we were hoping to promote. Through it, we hoped that they would experience a way of thinking and working that they could then share with their students. But initially we had to discover what concerns the teachers had that might serve as starting points for our action-based inquiry.

Changing Writing Conditions in Grade Three

The opportunity first came with the grade three teacher. Having been introduced to the idea of cooperative learning at a professional development day, Thomson decided to devote part of each Wednesday morning to a series of prestructured activities designed to develop the skills of cooperation. As this was a new way of working for her, she invited the researchers to participate and provide feedback on the experiment.

Over the six weeks of interchange, a working rapport developed between Thomson and Chang that facilitated the sharing of sensitive information, particularly about the connections between teacher beliefs, learning opportunities, and the children's participation. In her role as teacher, Thomson initially stressed preparation and planning as essential ingredients in the organization of group activities, being strongly influenced by her previous experience. However, in the light of Chang's observational insights, she began to stop and question or rethink her own practices and to formulate possible connections and disjunctions across the range of learning conditions she provided, such as between seatwork and activity-center work, and between cooperative group learning and children learning cooperatively in groups. These discussions, which took place after a half-day observation or on the telephone a day or two later, often led to a sharing of ideas on alternative practices, with discussion of potential outcomes and effects.

As a result of these exchanges, teacher and researcher gradually became more critical of their own ideas and roles. Thomson also became more open to the use of observational data as a way of revisiting phenomena to enable understanding to be more precise. Her growing epistemic stance towards research as a method for professional development moved from an initial examination of transcripts of audio data, through ethnographic analysis of observational data, to reading published papers on literacy in classroom contexts. Finally, in discussion with Wells, she agreed to allow video recordings to be made of teacher and researcher working with the children. This was an important development, for the role of reflective analysis of video data in the process of changing the conditions for learning hardly needs to be emphasized. Indeed, in our opinion, it was the evidence the video data provided of children's structures and strategies in these varied conditions that was the most significant factor in empowering Thomson to become an agent of curriculum change with respect to literacy and group work.

The dinosaur story-writing event, which we now wish to discuss, was one example of change. It was an important occasion in that, for the first time, Thomson allowed the children to take the initiative in deciding on group membership and the allocation of roles; she also allowed the groups to interpret the task for themselves; to write a story about dinosaurs based on what they had learned in their project work, to be shared with the rest of the class. After forty minutes of sustained group activity, their story read as follows:

Dinosaur School

Baby DINOSAURS Schools were in
VOCKANOS. Every 5 Years The
Fire Drial would Go On as an

ERUPTION. THEY WriHT About People.
THE Paper was 10 mters long. And
The Pencil is 5 mters long. There
Close is poka Doted. And THERE
Poget is about THE Fugter. THE
Librery is called Home read stone.
And The books or made of saled
Rock. THEY live in haya rock. THERE
Brians or as small as marbells.
THERE LUnCH is Brontobrgers. THERE TOYS
ARE all With Batreries. THERE HOUES is — MADE OF Pebulls.

—by Paulo, Maria, Carmina, Fei, and John.

Numerous studies of young children becoming literate from learning to write (e.g., Ferreiro and Teberosky 1982; Goelman, Oberg, and Smith 1984) have demonstrated the sociocognitive processes of children using writing for social interaction and for self-initiated expression, such as very young children using squiggles to mark ownership and labeling. However, more recent studies have been more concerned with demonstrating the reverse, i.e., children using interaction to develop the requisite sociocognitive-linguistic structures and procedures for writing (e.g., Dyson 1987; Heap 1986; Langer 1986). One strong claim made about the value of providing interactive writing events (such as co-authoring a story, teacher or peer conferencing, and letter or journal writing) is that these learning conditions expose children to alternative ways of composing, which in turn may facilitate their development of a personal composing model. Furthermore, when children are in conditions of writing that, in the course of responding as authors, call for justifications of the conceptual or rhetorical choices they make, they can meaningfully begin to revise their less effective composing skills and perhaps acquire new skills as well. In brief, interactive writing conditions enhance children's opportunities to become literate from learning to write. This we see demonstrated in more than one way in our video data of this particular writing condition.

The on-line talk that accompanied the writing of this text acts as a window on the children's writing processes. The first point we notice is that, like most writing tasks, the writing of this story represents a challenge to the writers to envision an audience. When Paulo, voted scribe for the group, initiates joint composing with "How about — er — You guys think too", the immediate responses of the co-writers are concerned with what would be interesting and entertaining for the reader. "It will be fun then," says Carmina. And this consideration appears to guide most of the suggestions made. In the case of this group of young writers, the alternatives take the form of titles—one common child strategy for topic identification and for making the boundaries of their meaning construction. After approximately twenty-five turns, the writers finally agree on "Dinosaur School." Their next task is to generate possible content.

J: The dinosaur school is back in time

P: No, the dinosaur school is underground

M: No, no

P: How about in a cave?

M: <u>No</u>

C: <u>No</u>

P: In a volcano?
(Group laughs)

C: In a volcano
(The children all speak at once)

M: Baby dinosaurs go to school

P: What?

M: Baby dinosaurs can go to—into a volcano for school

C: Baby dinosaur

P: Cor—

J: Then they put a bomb inside the volcano

P: Then we try to put in tyrannosaurus rex? Get it?
He wrecks everything

Evidently, these young writers first give their attention to finding a suitable starting idea rather than to deciding how the story should begin. Their child-driven strategy for accessing appropriate content is based, not on the consideration of what elements would constitute an effective beginning and the goals for one, but on generating ideas that their co-writers might like. In cases of expert writers co-authoring a text interactively, the response of either to what has been written is both audience-like and a judgment of whether negotiated intentions and goals have been met. However, the third graders' process-talk is quite different from that of expert co-writers. For example, in making their proposals for the topic title, they act as if they have already established intentions and goals, so no discussion is necessary. Taking this assumption as tacit underpins the children's approach to joint composing, quite unlike that of expert writers.

The five third graders co-authoring "Dinosaur School" demon-strate not only their abilities for social self-expression, but also their growing understanding of the influence of the audience on the composing process: the orientation to others within one's constructive efforts when thinking and writing (Heap 1986). Indeed, it is the children's move beyond initial response to a word, phrase, or sentence written, to engagement with ideas, that is remarkable in the following dialogue.

P: Baby dinosaur schools are in — are in . volcanos

M: <u>WERE in</u>

J: <u>WERE in</u>

M: They are not right now. Are dinosaurs living right now? 'were' (repeating as Paulo writes)

P: But this is make believe.

M: I didn't realize there's — there's really a dinosaur school

Another instance occurs when Maria reads aloud what Paulo is scribing and, noticing an inconsistency, she remarks:

M: Hm you put dinosaur
       DinoSAURS (emphasizing the plural form)

P: I can't do anything now

J: What did he do wrong?

M: Dinosaur he put. dinoSAURS (again emphasizing the plural) like thousands of them . more than one

P: So — so that's what the school is

M: A school with one kid (laughs)

C: Dinosaur school . school of one kid

Here, we have evidence of the children's spontaneous willingness to explain, to question their own ideas in writing, and to play out the hypothetical consequences of alternatives suggested in order to help the writer in understanding what the text says and what it means, each time any of them is, so to speak, the writer. The role of writer moves fluidly from child to child, each taking control of the composition when it is his or her self-initiated turn.

A final example confirms this point. Maria's first suggestion for the second sentence is "Every five hundred years the fire drill will go on as an eruption." However, when this is objected to, she modifies her suggestion.

M: Yeah five years . because they won't be alive in five hundred years

J: Yes they would

M: But they wouldn't be babies any more

P: Yeah

C: They'll be five

J: So they'll be in grade six

M: They are in grade six,   they'll be in high school . they'll be teenagers
   . not babies any more

From the interactive nature of the cycle of response to something
written and feedback on an alternative suggested, we begin to witness
the children's emerging ability to revise when provided with appropriate conditions to do so. We believe that numerous occasions
of this kind of literacy condition will certainly nourish the recognition that writing in school does not have to be a completion of an
assigment that is effortful and ill-understood. Instead, it can be an
enjoyable and meaningful event that enables the writer to draw
upon and develop the various skills needed to compose a text that
is to be understood by varied and unconvinced audiences.

Relating Science and Literacy in Grade Five

Several times during the year, Michael Dougherty had expressed
his interest in teaching science in the junior grades. In the spring,
he decided to devote a considerable amount of class time to the
theme of energy, with the children working in self-selected groups
on projects of their own choosing. A number of factors led to this
decision, including an upcoming parents' evening at which he
wished the children to have work to display, the talk about group
work in the staff room, reading about another class in which similar
theme-based work had been successful (see chapter 3), and discussions on issues of literacy, learning, and language with the
researchers. From the beginning, he was keen that the researchers'
participation should extend beyond observation and videotaping,
as he felt that to have other knowledgeable adults in the classroom
would be of benefit, since there would be many groups simultaneously needing assistance.

   He was correct in this judgment, and over the next month,
Dougherty and Chang spent a considerable amount of time talking
with various groups about their projects, helping them to clarify,
plan, review, and revise their intentions as they worked towards
their chosen outcomes. Wells's visits were less frequent and were
mainly devoted to videotaping, but on occasions he, too, worked
with various groups.

   Beside being facilitators of the small groups, Dougherty, Chang,
and Wells used the frequent discussions they had together to enable
each other to work jointly towards Dougherty's intention of developing a community of speakers and audiences among his fifth
graders. But the more significant literacy objective with which the
study of energy became integrated was that of empowering the

children to take intentional control over their own thinking. To achieve this change was indeed a challenge, as Dougherty began to conceptualize the children's learning experiences and develop a new way of thinking about the connection between science, literacy, and language development. For these aims, Wells and Chang acted as catalysts and participant observers of the children working to know and learn, and the insights thus gained were the elements for establishing the collaborative relationship with Dougherty.

All ten groups of fifth graders were introduced to the idea of using the library as a resource center, especially during the topic identification phase of their projects. Consequently, reading played a major role in almost every group's approach to their topic, as they sought out the information needed to formulate a feasible question for investigation. The role envisaged for writing was initially quite small but, through the group discussions, the children were alerted to the varied and important functions that writing could perform in carrying out their projects. However, for this paper we will focus our analysis of the video data on the structures and strategies that the children shared through talk as they moved from information externally located in people and books to personal understanding — in other words, on how these fifth graders constructed knowledge under the learning conditions of group investigation.

Judith, Suyin, Vanda, and Teresa were working on wind energy. Following a lengthy conference with Chang and Wells, Judith was asked by her teacher to share with the rest of the class the strategies her group had learned to use.

J: We'll be doing about the history of the windmills, and like what they used the windmills for and we will . . .
The sheet here of what we know about the windmills and what we need to find out . .
So we'll be doing that and we're doing a model and sheets so we won't have to do much job . Ok?

D: Did you discover any special problems that you'll have to do — you will have to work on?

J: What do you mean "special"?

D: Well . while you were making an outline of things that you know and things that you have to find out did you come across anything that — any part of it that's particularly difficult?

V: Now we have to find out how we're going to make it [the model]

J: Yeah

D: The actual construction?

J: Yeah . It is to do — I don't know . We're not sure about size yet

D: So you've got — so did you outline then the things you'll be needing?

J: Yeah

As can be seen in this extract, ·the teacher's monitoring of the children working in a group provided occasions for making small group talk a part of the learning process, and using public articulation as a learning tool. Whenever the fifth graders had to explain, report, justify, and illustrate their progress and the directions their investigations would be taking, not only did their knowledge on energy increase, but also the explicit and logical processes that underlay the articulation of their ideas became more public. When both teacher and children were aware of this, and intentionally developed these processes, we observed the children reflecting and analyzing in terms of distinctions like "what we know" and "what we need to find out".

The location of inconsistencies or gaps, expressed as special problems, is an example of the problem-solving framework that was being fostered, within which the children might conceptualize their inquiries. However, this mode of thinking about constraints encountered was still unfamiliar, as is evidenced by Judith's question: "What do you mean 'special'?" Nonetheless, this does not mean that the young researchers were without their own strategies for problem solving. To the children, "the sheets" represented a documentation of their planning, monitoring, and revising of their issues, of work to be done and how it should be done. Examination of this tangible trace of the children's thoughts concerning their project indicates a systematicity in their construction of hypotheses, and in their categorization and reshaping of information taken from books according to their self-defined criteria.

So far, we have pointed to the literacy benefits that accrue when children are encouraged to make their group discussions and decisions public. Another literacy condition that was consistently fostered throughout this unit of science study was the request to share the group's findings and what each individual or the group as a whole had learned. This does not refer only to the presentation of final outcomes. It includes the sharing of results so far achieved, the examination of different aspects of the topic from a variety of perspectives, and the up dating of their current understanding of the investigation.

For example, among our video data are extracts from the various stages of learning that a group of four boys experienced in their joint construction of a model of a windmill. Having to address issues such as the relationships among various types of energy, and problems such as the measurement and synchronization of gears and parts of the model, Wen Kai, Jethro, Peter, and Kim Hock came to understand the significance of theoretical knowledge. Like all enthusiastic youngsters engaging in projects, the four fifth graders initially thought that their commonsense thinking would be sufficient to carry out their chosen task. However, making a windmill to illustrate the operation of wind energy became a learning experience that tested in observable phenomena the applicability of their lay knowledge. This had profound literate consequences for the boys. They began to recognize the difference between "commonsense knowledge" and "theoretical knowledge" when tested in the tasks that they undertook.

For example, these young researchers were confronted with the task of meshing two cogwheels to drive the gear shaft that turned the grinding stone in their windwill. First, they realized their investigation had moved from wind energy to mechanical energy and, second, they discovered that their commonsense knowledge about how to cut two circular pieces of tin to form the cogwheels was inadequate. Reference to theoretical knowledge such as the weight of the wheels in proportion to the weight of the shaft and grinding stone also had to be considered for the wheels to function. Indeed, the thinking processes as well as the desire to make use of reference books that were generated in this context hardly need to be elaborated.

Conclusion

We began this chapter by arguing that it is in the activity of writing that the nature of literacy is most readily grasped and the potential of language for empowering thinking most fully experienced. For it is through engaging in the cyclical processes of composing and interpretation that any sustained piece of writing requires that writers come both to understand their subject and recognize the limits of their understanding. Through engaging in these same processes in a reflective manner, they can also learn to take intentional control of their own thinking. At the same time, it has to be recognized that goals such as these do not usually figure prominently in the teaching of literacy in the early school years. It is for these reasons that we have focused on writing in our examination of the attempts to change the conditions for literacy learning in these two classrooms.

However, as the evidence shows, to focus on writing need not be restricting. On the contrary, when writing is treated as a powerful means of thinking and communicating in the service of coming to know and to understand substantive matters, the development of writing ability and the acquisition of domain knowledge will *both* be enhanced. For this to happen, though, writing needs to be conceived as a means for the development of literate thinking. We recognize, of course, that the data cited fall far short of substantiating our claim that such a development was taking place. However, our aims were as much to investigate the change process itself and the means by which that change came about, as to demonstrate the results seen in terms of the children's performance. Nevertheless, we believe we have been able to demonstrate the uncovering of the children's potential.

An equally important aim was to develop a framework for conceptualizing the relationship between writing and the construction of domain knowledge that would have both research and educational applicability. In fact, an earlier version of the model of an inquiry-centered curriculum, presented at the end of the previous chapter, was the outcome of this attempt. Certainly, we found the emerging model helped us to see connections between the kinds of literate thinking in which the third and fifth graders were being encouraged to engage and the evolution that was taking place in the teachers' own thinking. To be sure, the structure of the model and the language in which it is articulated emerged out of the ongoing discussion and after-the-event reflection, rather than being prepared in advance for delivery to the teachers. Yet it is precisely this hindsight cognition that is our strongest evidence of the gains attained by teachers and researchers, and also by the children, in the act of changing the learning conditions to those that reflect a concept of literacy that empowers minds.

Chapter Seven

Talk About Text
Where Literacy is Learned and Taught

My aim in this final chapter is to bring together the major themes of the preceding chapters in a discussion of the nature of literacy as I have come to understand it, of its development both at school and in the pre-school years, and of the role that talk about texts plays in that development. I also want to say something about teachers learning how to promote the development of literacy through the inquiries that they carry out in their own classrooms and about the role that talk about texts of a different kind plays in their learning. In discussing both students' and teachers' learning, I shall be adopting the sociocultural perspective, developed in chapter 2, that sees learning as the appropriation and transformation of the resources of the culture in order to achieve goals that are both personally and socially defined. Let me start with a discussion of literacy and, more specifically, with a sketch of the historical development of written language.

Literacy: A Technology for the Empowerment of Mind

Of course, we cannot be sure what the origins of written language were but, almost certainly, writing was used very early as a form of external memory for information of practical importance. For example, in order to preserve them for future use, oil, wine, corn, and so on, would be stored in sealed clay vessels. Initially, someone would have to remember what was in the different jars or, in the absence of such a person, the jars would have to be opened at random in order to discover what was inside. Marking a symbol on the outside of the pot relieved this burden on memory — provided that the symbols used could be interpreted according to some shared conventions. Similarly, written symbols were used to record taxes paid or owing, or to list valuable possessions.[13] For practical reasons of this kind, a number of civilizations independently invented ways of giving systematic visual representation to linguistic meaning — based on morphemes, syllables, or phonemes. But, whatever the basis of the relationship between linguistic meaning and visual symbol, the crucial feature that all these systems had in common was that, in contrast to speech, they allowed meaning to be preserved beyond the point of utterance. That is to say, for the first time, they enabled meaning to be represented in a medium that was permanent — or at least relatively so.

Once the significance of this characteristic of the written text had been grasped, the use of the new technology expanded into other areas. And as the range of uses expanded, so did the techniques and conventions of representation. To the principle of alphabetization, first found in a complete form in the Greek script, were gradually added constant directionality, spacing between words, paragraphing, pagination, tables of contents, indexes, and so on, all of which greatly increased the possibility of the written text coming to function as a freestanding representation of meaning, independent of the intentions in the mind of the writer at the time of writing and of the particular context in which it was produced or to which it originally referred (Morrison 1987).

It was this context-independent permanence of written texts that made the invention of writing such an important cultural achievement. For, in addition to the capturing of information of a purely practical kind, it made possible the preservation and accumulation of discursive information on a wide variety of topics far beyond what a single individual could discover and remember for him- or herself. Thus, by exploiting this archival function of writing (Olson 1977) — by systematically collating, comparing, and organizing the texts produced by others — scholars over time gradually established the textual basis of the subject disciplines that we know today. Indeed, it is no exaggeration to say that, without some form of permanent, external, conventional system for representing meaning, the achievements of modern science and technology would be inconceivable — as would serious study in any of the humanistic disciplines. (For thorough discussions of the historical development of literacy in Western societies and of its consequences for ways of thinking, see Goody [1977] and Ong [1982].)

But the sheer accumulation of information does not in itself lead to knowledge. For knowledge, being a state of understanding achieved through constructive mental effort, requires the individual to engage with the relevant texts in a critical and creative manner in an attempt to bring about a correspondence between the meaning represented in the text and the meaning represented in the mind (Flower 1987). And it is this latter function of written language — as a medium through which individuals, through the interrogation of their own or others' texts, can extend their own thinking and understanding — that led Bruner, speaking at a recent conference on orality and literacy, to characterize literacy as "a technology for the empowerment of mind".

A Model of Literacy: Text Types and Modes of Engagement

The foregoing history of written language is, of course, incomplete. For example, I have neglected to say anything about the social aspects of literacy — its function in creating communities of like-minded thinkers and the role it has played in the development of such institutions as religion and the law (Stock 1983). Nor, on the other hand, have I considered the cultural conflicts that have frequently accompanied the spread of literacy, as powerful elites, whether colonial or indigenous, have attempted to impose their particular form of literacy on less powerful groups, who were either preliterate or whose literacy practices were based on less highly valued forms of literacy (Street 1987). Instead, my intention has been to emphasize certain intellectual functions that written language has gradually come to perform, in order to propose a more general account of literacy in contemporary Western society, based on a model which distinguishes five different modes of engaging with written texts. While no claim is made for their exhaustiveness, the five modes represent, I believe, the broad categories of engagement that are most frequently required in everyday life in our society; as such, they are proposed as a basis for considering the learning and teaching of literacy in relation to the school curriculum.[14]

Every written text has a physical form — marks inscribed on a surface that represent the writer's meanings according to the conventions of a linguistic code. When the user of a text focuses on the code — on the encoding/decoding relationship between meaning and its physical representation, and the conventions that govern it — I shall talk about this as engaging with the text in the *performative* mode. This is the mode we adopt, for example, when we are proofreading something we have written or when we are skimming through a telephone directory, looking for a particular entry. Of necessity, beginning readers and writers have to devote a considerable amount of their attention to learning how to use the code. However, even for them, a concern with form is rarely the primary purpose. Competence in the performative mode is therefore best seen as a means to engaging with the text in other modes; as long as that competence is adequate for the purpose at hand, it normally functions below the level of conscious attention.

The second mode of engagement that I wish to distinguish has its origins in the very first uses of written language. This I shall call the *functional* mode. In this mode, we treat the text as an adjunct or means to the achievement of some other purpose as, for example, when using the appropriate form to pay money into the bank, consulting a timetable to plan a journey, leaving instructions for another family member on what to prepare for dinner, or finding out from the instruction manual how to use a recently acquired machine. In these contexts, we engage with the various texts in order to act, and the text functions instrumentally as a means to that end.

The third mode of engagement I shall call the *informational*. In this mode we treat the text as a channel by means of which information is communicated from one person to another. The validity or significance of the information being communicated is not at issue; rather, the focus is on accuracy of comprehension or on clarity and conciseness of expression. Consulting a reference book to find out the facts on a question or to identify an unknown flower or bird would be examples of this mode of engagement, as would writing a routine report or completing a questionnaire.

In the fourth mode, by contrast, the text is engaged with as a verbal artifact. In calling this mode the *re-creational*, I intend to capture the sense of engagement with the text being an end in itself, undertaken for the pleasure of constructing and exploring a world through words, whether one's own or those of another author. While much of our reading of imaginative literature is undertaken in this mode, other genres can also be read in the same way; this is also likely to be the mode in which we write "expressively" (Britton et al. 1975), for example, in letters to friends or entries in a personal journal.[15]

Important though each of these modes of engagement is in the course of everyday life, however, none fully exploits the potential of written text as this was described at the end of the previous section. For that, we need to introduce a fifth mode of engagement, which I shall call the *epistemic*, from the Greek word for knowledge. In this mode, the text is treated, not as a representation of meaning that is already decided, given, and self-evident, but as a tentative and provisional attempt on the part of the writer to capture his or her current understanding in an external form so that it may provoke further attempts at understanding as the writer or some other reader dialogues with the text in order to interpret its meaning (Lotman 1988). Any text *can* be read in this way, though some texts are much more likely than others to elicit this mode of engagement; these might include works of philosophy, poetry, scientific research reports, legal argument, and so on. *All* serious and sustained acts of written composition, on the other hand — as will be argued below — demand an epistemic mode of engagement.

When one reads what someone else has written in order to try to understand what it can mean; when one considers alternative possible interpretations and looks for internal evidence to choose between them; when one asks, Is the text internally consistent? and Does it make sense in relation to my own experience? one is engaging with the text epistemically — even when reading a text that one has written oneself. However, there is an important difference between reading and writing in terms of the contribution that each makes to the construction of knowledge. In the course of reading one may see connections between things one already knows or achieve insights of feeling and understanding that go beyond the already known. Unfortunately, however, the mental representations created through reading fade almost as quickly as those created in the course of oral communication, and even rereading provides no guarantee of recapturing them.

It is here that writing is so powerful. For, by writing them down, one can capture those insights and perceived connections so that they can be returned to, critically examined, reconsidered, and perhaps made the basis for the construction of a further sustained text of one's own. And, in the creation of one's own text, one is forced to go even further in the development of one's understanding. At all stages in its creation, one is involved in a variety of constructive mental processes: assessing what one knows about the topic and what one does not yet know that one needs to come to know; selecting what is relevant from this knowledge for the purpose in hand; and organizing and expressing it in the form most appropriate to achieve this purpose with respect to the intended audience. Sustained writing on any topic of importance to the writer thus involves a fruitful dialectic between what Scardamalia and Bereiter (1985) refer to as "the content space and the rhetorical space". Furthermore, since each attempt to resolve that dialectic through the construction of a particular text leaves a record in the form of a working draft, one can return to the draft as one's own first critical reader to discover what it means and then work to revise it and, through both processes, extend one's understanding of the topic about which one is writing (Murray 1978; 1982).

This then, is the empowerment that comes from engaging with texts epistemically, whether as reader or writer (but particularly as writer) by conducting the transaction between the representation on the page and the representation in the head, one can make advances in one's intellectual, moral, or affective understanding to an extent that would otherwise be difficult or impossible to achieve. To be *fully* literate, therefore, is to have both the ability and the disposition to engage with texts epistemically when the occasion demands.

Although they can be seen as being of differential significance for the intellectual development of individuals and of the societies of which they are members, the five modes of engaging with texts that I have just outlined should be thought of as complementary with respect to the range of purposes that written language serves, rather than as mutually exclusive. Moreover, it is important to emphasize that any text can be engaged with in any of the five modes, and that during a complete literacy event, one may move between modes, with each mode supporting and facilitating the others. Indeed, I have just argued that any sustained piece of writing will almost necessarily involve an epistemic mode of engagement and this will demand engagement in one or more of the other modes at appropriate points for its full achievement. This relationship is shown here:

Nevertheless, there is a strong tendency for texts of any particular type to elicit a dominant mode of engagement — particularly in the case of reading — by virtue of the function that that type of text is designed to serve in the lives of those who engage with it. Reference books, for example, are most commonly read to obtain information, TV guides consulted to organize viewing, checks written to pay bills, and so on. The extent and quality of a person's literacy will thus be strongly influenced by the types of text that he or she most frequently encounters as reader or writer, since this will tend to determine which modes of engagement are most frequently practiced.[16]

This being so, it is worth pausing for a moment to consider the types of written text that students most frequently encounter in school. For the relative emphasis that is given to different types of text and to the purposes for which students are expected to engage with them must surely be important in shaping the concepts of the nature and value of literacy that they gradually construct in the processes of reading and writing.

Reading and Writing Texts in the Classroom

For the purposes of argument, let me propose a rather crude four-way classification of the types of text that are found in abundance in almost all schools as a starting point for such an investigation.[17] First, there is the basal reading series, with all its associated exercises and worksheets, the prime purpose of which is to instruct the student in the use of the conventions of the written code. Second, there are the notices displayed at various points around the school, instructing visitors to report to the office, students not to run in the corridors, and so on. In individual classrooms are also to be found texts of the same basic type concerning the feeding of classroom pets, due dates and times for the completion of work. The third category consists of the textbooks that are the basic resource for the teaching of most subjects in the curriculum; into this category also fall the reference books of various kinds that are used as supplementary material. The final category, by constrast, is much more heterogeneous and is to be found in the school or classroom library and in the desks, cupboards, and tote-bags of individual students. What characterizes the texts in this fourth category is that, by and large, they were written, not by a committee with the deliberate intention of shaping people's beliefs and behaviors, but by individual authors who cared enough about their topics to want, through words, to create worlds to be explored, delighted in, and reflected upon.

From the growing number of observational studies in classrooms, we can predict with some confidence the pattern of relationships that is likely to hold between these four categories of texts and the five modes of engagement that I outlined earlier. The basal reading series, being predominantly concerned with providing instruction in the skills involved in reading and writing, tends to emphasize the performative mode of engagement, with a secondary emphasis on the informational. Although the stories and poems that such readers contain could be engaged with re-creationally and epistemically, actual observation suggests that this rarely occurs; instead, the emphasis is, first, on accurately reading the text aloud and then on correctly answering factual questions by locating the information in the text or by drawing the inferences from related real-world knowledge that are culturally warranted (Heap 1985). The second category of texts, being concerned to regulate action, tends to elicit a functional mode of engagement. Interestingly, however, although it is "functional literacy" (or illiteracy) that is at the forefront of concern about falling standards in schools, such action-oriented texts, and the associated functional mode of engagement, are rarely given explicit attention in school; it is presumably assumed that, being so ubiquitous, such texts are unproblematic.

For text and reference books, the dominant mode of engagement tends to be the informational. Such instructional texts, being designed in general to transmit the culturally sanctioned facts and values of a given subject area in an orderly and predetermined sequence, assume — or are ascribed — an authority which militates against the questioning and critical stance that characterizes the epistemic mode of engagement (Olson 1980; Luke, de Castell and Luke 1983). To a considerable extent, the same emphasis on an informational mode of engagement characterizes the students' written assignments that are based on the study of instructional texts (Britton et al. 1975). Produced to demonstrate adequate and accurate absorption of the required information, such student texts show little tendency to speculate, to question the established view, or to offer alternative perspectives.

For the category of what might be called "real" books, it is difficult to say with confidence what mode of engagement they elicit. If their authors were consulted, they would no doubt say that their intention was to engage their readers re-creationally and, hopefully, also epistemically. However, when novels and other works of literature are selected for class study, in high school as well as in elementary school, they are all too often subverted for purposes similar to those that typify the use of the basal reader, with an emphasis on literal comprehension and the drawing of inferences predetermined by the teacher (Baker and Freebody 1989). Similarly, students' own extended writing of an imaginative or discursive kind is, by the way in which it is responded to by the teacher, frequently reduced to an occasion for attention to spelling, punctuation, and the avoidance of stylistic solecisms.

Where, then, do students have the opportunity to engage with texts in a re-creational or epistemic mode within the prescribed curriculum? The answer is that, in many classrooms, there is little or no such opportunity. Of course, this does not mean that students do not engage in re-creational reading and, to a lesser extent, writing, but only in the few minutes before recess when they have finished the "real" work, or in their own time outside the classroom. On occasion, too, when their own purposes demand it, they may adopt an epistemic mode of engagement. But as the direct focus of teacher and student concern, classroom activities in which a re-creational mode of engagement with texts is deliberately planned are still all too rare, and those in which the epistemic mode is given systematic attention are even rarer (Baird, in press).

Exactly where the relative emphasis falls obviously varies from teacher to teacher. But there is sufficient evidence from classroom research to suggest that, despite the impressive statements of aims to be found in policy documents, the transmission-oriented curriculum that actually operates in many classrooms — at all levels of education — has the effect of constraining both the range of text types that are given explicit attention and the opportunities to engage with texts of any type in ways that encourage those characteristics of critical and constructive thinking that I have called epistemic.

Some will no doubt reply that epistemic literacy is indeed the goal towards which they are striving, but that it is premature to attempt to get students to engage with texts in that mode until they have mastered the prerequisite skills and accumulated the necessary information. In effect, what they are proposing is another version of the pedagogical fallacy that equates the developmental sequence of learning with the abstract hierarchy of skills that is used to organize instruction. However, in learning to talk, children do not first learn lexical items and the syntactic structures in which to combine them, and only then use these linguistic resources to interact with other people and to learn about the world. By the same token, in learning to be literate, they do not need to have fully mastered the code and the information contained in the text in order to begin to interact with it epistemically. Indeed, just the reverse. For it is when children understand, from shared story reading, that texts are representations of worlds waiting to be explored, challenged, and even improved upon, that they will be most strongly motivated to master the performative mode of engagement so that they can read them for themselves (Wells 1986). Similarly, when students in school are encouraged to treat texts not as authoritative pronouncements but as contributions to an ongoing dialogue in which they can be active participants in the search for understanding, they will be more inclined to acquire the range of skills and strategies that are necessary for full participation.

It cannot be too strongly emphasized, therefore, that the five modes of engaging with text proposed here should *not* be construed as constituting a developmental sequence. Rather, they should be seen as forming a repertoire of complementary approaches to texts, all of which need to be given deliberate attention at every stage of literacy development. Moreover, since the epistemic mode of engagement with texts subsumes all the other modes, it should be seen, not as a distant and unattainable goal, but as the most effective point of entry for literacy learning and as the focus for each unit of work at every level of education. For if students are to discover the potential that literacy has to empower their thinking, feeling, and action—in other words, if they are to become fully literate—they must engage with texts in this way at *all* stages in their development. How this can be achieved will be the burden of the latter half of this chapter. But first I want to extend the definition of "text".

Texts as Symbolic Representations

What is important about a text, I suggested earlier, is that it is an external and permanent linguistic representation of the meanings intended by its producer. But, if that is so, there are surely other modes in which these objectives can be achieved, such as in algebraic equations or in scientific formulae. In fact, there is no problem with treating these forms as texts, for in each case they are representations couched in a conventional language. Then what about a diagram, a flow chart, or a musical score? Here, too, there seems to be no difficulty in extending the notion of text to cover them as, in each case, they employ an explicit and conventional symbolic system. But what about a painting or a model? These must be more controversial since, although they are symbolic representations, the conventions in terms of which they are created are much less explicit. Nevertheless, I want to suggest that it is heuristically worthwhile to extend the notion of text to any artifact that is constructed as a representation of meaning using a conventional symbolic system. For, by virtue of its permanence and the symbolic mode in which it is created, any such artifact performs the essential function of allowing us to create an external, fixed representation of the sense we make of our experience so that we may reflect upon and manipulate it.

Having come this far, it is only a small step to recognizing the existence of another class of potential texts, which are around us all the time in the form of oral discourse. With the invention of the tape recorder, it has become possible to capture episodes of talk in a permanent form so that they, too, can be reheard and reviewed in very much the same way as written texts. Of course, the practice of recording important speech events in writing has a long history in such forms as court records or in notes taken in lectures. But it is only the advent of the tape recorder that has made it possible to capture verbatim the utterances actually spoken.

However, even before the invention of electronic recording devices—or even of writing—there were ways of making speech memorable so that it achieved a sort of permanence that made it potentially available for reflection. The most obvious examples are the great oral epics, such as Homer's *Iliad*, which were clearly texts in the sense in which I have defined the term and, no doubt, on occasion they elicited the sort of engagement that we should recognize as epistemic.

But there is little doubt that it was as a result of the growing pervasiveness of written texts in all aspects of life that the literate practice of distinguishing the form of the message—the text—from the intentions of its producer was carried over to the spoken mode of communication so that, when the occasion demands, literate people can give the same sort of critical attention to oral texts as they habitually give to texts in the written mode. And it is probably this practice, as much as the shared engagement with written texts, that provides the introduction to literacy for those children who grow up in highly literate homes.

In a recent discussion of pre-school experiences that prepare children for the literacy demands of school, Heath (1986) has developed this idea by identifying a number of such "oral literacy events" that is to say, events in which what is said is made the focus of attention (see chapter 4). One of the categories that she discusses is the "recount," which is the sort of text that might be produced when a small child and one parent have returned from a visit to the park or the local supermarket, and the accompanying parent asks the child to tell the other parent about the visit. Under such conditions, the child's recounting of what happened is likely to be closely monitored for its accuracy and completeness and, where necessary, corrected or extended, with the result that the child is in effect invited to monitor his or her oral rendition in very much the same way as one might treat the draft of a written text.

Other oral events that invite the same attention to the form as well as the content of what is said can be found in the show-and-tell time that is so common in the primary grades, or in the academic lecture or the contributions to a debate. What I want to suggest, therefore, is that, with or without the aid of a tape recorder, there is quite a wide variety of events during which close attention is given to the actual words spoken, as well as to the speaker's intentions, so that it is appropriate to extend the notion of text to include such oral productions within its scope.

So, having arrived at a working definition of a text, we can use this and the notion of different modes of engagement with texts to attempt a tentative and provisional characterization of what it is to be literate. *To be literate is to have the disposition to engage appropriately with texts of different types in order to empower action, thinking, and feeling in the context of purposeful social activity.*[18]

Literacy Learning as a Cultural Apprenticeship

To define literacy in dispositional terms is to emphasize the *use* of the relevant skills as well as their possession. And it is a similar emphasis on learning through meaningful use that lies behind Smith's (1983) characterization of learning to read and write as "joining the literacy club." Youngsters, he suggests, learn to read by reading, and to write by writing, in the company of fully paid-up club members whose own behavior provides demonstrations both of what is worth doing and of how to do it. Another way of putting this is to say that becoming literate is best seen in terms of an apprenticeship, in which the learner is inducted into the model of literacy implicitly held by the more expert performer. And in an earlier paper (Wells 1987), I showed how differences in success in literacy learning in school, which are found in a wide variety of cultures, could be accounted for by the socially based differences in the value given to different types of text and modes of engaging with them that learners encounter in their communities as well as in their classrooms.

Learning through apprenticeship is, in fact, a universal phenomenon and is the normal mode through which most cultural practices are acquired. Described by Rogoff and colleagues (forthcoming) as "guided participation in situations of joint involvement with other people in culturally important activities," it is what Vygotsky (1978) had in mind in his well-known exposition of "learning in the zone of proximal development". In his view, all cultural knowledge, and, indeed, the higher mental processes themselves, are acquired through social interaction as, in the course of shared participation in a joint activity, the more mature member of the culture, while enacting the total process, draws the novice into participation and gradually allows him or her to take over more and more of the task, as he or she shows the ability to do so.

In many of the instances of cultural learning that have so far been studied, it is clear that it is from demonstration and guided hands-on performance that the child gradually appropriates the relevant behavior (that is to say the child learns why and how to perform the constituent actions). However, these forms of collaboration are most appropriate for cultural practices of a predominantly physical kind, such as kneading dough, tying shoelaces, or weaving on a handloom (Rogoff 1990). In the case of less predominantly physical activities, such as reading or writing, they seem less likely to be sufficient. Indeed, since these literate practices are, as we have just seen, essentially a matter of engaging with a particular text in a manner appropriate to one's goals on a particular occasion, it is difficult to see how such essentially *mental* abilities could be acquired by simply observing an expert's overt behavior. Equally, it is of little value to guide the novice's action if he or she has no understanding of the significance of the action to the overall goal of the activity. What this means, therefore, is that in the case of such cultural practices as those associated with literacy, talk in and about the activity can no longer remain an optional aspect of the collaboration, as in the case of such practices as weaving or baking, but must be seen as both central and essential.

Consider, as an example, such a familiar shared literacy practice as a parent and child choosing grocery items from the shelves on a shopping expedition to the local supermarket. In this context, the adult's silent reading of the labels on the packets would not be transparently meaningful (nor probably even observable) to a youngster who did not know that the symbols on the outside of the packets corresponded to the contents on the inside and that the differences between the configurations of symbols were systematically and conventionally related to differences between the spoken words that are used to differentially label the contents. In practice, of course, adults who want their children to learn from this shared activity not only read the labels aloud but also verbally draw attention to the salient symbols on the labels and the nature of the contents; they probably also offer explanations of what they are doing.

It is for this reason that, although I agree with Smith on the importance he attaches to children learning to read and write by reading and writing real texts for purposes that are personally meaningful to them, I want to emphasize the importance of such occasions occurring in the context of *joint* literacy events, in which the significance of the literate behavior is *made overt through talk*. It is preeminently in such verbally-mediated assisted performance, (in talk about text) that literacy is learned and taught.

In the next section of this chapter, therefore, a number of examples of talk about text will be examined in an attempt to discover precisely what kinds of opportunities for becoming literate they provide. First, we shall consider some typical literacy events observed in the home; then we shall look at some examples of talk about text in the classroom.

Talk About Text at Home and School

The first example, which is taken from Tizard and Hughes's (1984) study of four-year-old girls at home and at nursery school, concerns the revision of a shopping list. Pauline's mother is crossing off her list the items that her neighbor has just offered to bring back for her from the local store. Pauline, on the other hand, has a further item that she wants to add to the list.

M: We've only got that little bit of shopping to get now [shows Pauline the list].

C: Mummy? Can I have one of them drinks? Can I?

M: Get some more drink?

C: Yeah. Can write it down on there [points to where she wants it written on the list]. Up here.

M: I'll get you some when I go tomorrow.

C: Aw! [disappointed]

M: All right? 'Cause I'm not getting it today.

C: No ... In in the 'Vivo's'? [the local store]

M: Haven't got Daddy's money yet.
[For several turns they discuss the need to have enough money to pay for all the items]

C: Mum, let's have a look! [Mother shows child the list]
Do it again.

M: We gotta get rice, tea, braising steak, cheese, pickle, carrots, fish, chicken, bread, eggs, bacon, beefburgers, beans ... Oh, Irene's gone to get them [crosses off beans] ... peas, ham, corned beef.

C: And what's that? [points to a word on the list]

M: That's lemon drink [crosses off lemon drink] She's just gone down to get that one. See? (pp. 74–75)

Commenting on this episode, Tizard and Hughes write, "a shopping list provides an extremely vivid demonstration of the way in which written language may be used within a meaningful human activity. The power of the written word lies in its ability to link up different contexts in space or time, and here it is doing precisely that — forming a link between the home, where the decisions and choices are made, and the shop, where they are carried out" (p. 76). And it is precisely because of its embeddedness in the routines of everyday life that this episode is so effective in pointing up this link. For not only are the items that are included in the list meaningful in terms of Pauline's knowledge of the ingredients used in the preparation of meals and snacks, but she is also made aware of the practical constraints on the inclusion of items: "Haven't got Daddy's money yet." At the same time, she is allowed to participate in the construction of the list by requesting an item for inclusion, but with her mother doing the actual writing in the place that Pauline has designated.

Put in terms of the broad categories introduced earlier, this event clearly involves an action-oriented text; equally clearly, the dominant mode of engagement with the text is functional. And it is the specific functional connection between text and action—the relationship between the structure and the content of this list and the particular objects and actions in the practical world to which it is related—that is pointed up in the talk in which the items to be included are negotiated. This is what is made available for learning here and Pauline shows that she has indeed achieved some grasp of the function of the text when she asks her mother to add a drink for her to the list. But, as in most literacy events, the functional is not the only mode of engagement that is called into play. When Pauline's mother writes on the list, and again when Pauline asks about a particular word on the list, it is the performative mode that is brought into focus. Through close attention to specific entries on the list, matching the visual display with the encoded meaning, she is also meeting the evidence that over many such occasions, will allow her to construct a representation of the written code itself and of how to use it. As in most naturally occurring literacy events, however, the performative mode of engagement remains instrumental: the actual acts of reading and writing are means to the achievement of a larger purpose.

My second example comes from a study of shared book reading by Sulzby and Teale (1987). In this episode, Hannah (26 months old) and her mother are reading a label book called *Baby Animals.*

M: (reading) 'Kittens are baby cats.'

H: Tha— ... that's the mommy cat?

M: The mommy is the cat; the babies are kittens.
Can you say kittens?

H: Kittens.

M: That's right. Kittens.

H: It's ... up here. (pointing to the back and tail of a kitten that can be seen over the back of the basket in the picture)

M: Is that ... that's the back end of a baby kitten, isn't it? And there's his ear sticking up. See? Is that his ear?

H: (nods)

M: What's he playing in?

H: In yarn.

M: Is he playing in the yarn basket?

H: Yes. See? (laughing) (p. 59)

Here we have a composite text, consisting of pictures and brief statements that label or comment on the pictures. Not surprisingly, given Hannah's age, it is the pictures that occupy most of her attention. But, as can be seen in this brief extract, the two modalities of the composite text work together, the words cueing the way in which the picture should be understood, and the picture providing a (two-dimensional) referent for the words. And this is how the mother enacts the event with Hannah, first explaining the definitional statement through expansion and then, in response to Hannah's observation, going on to discuss some of the details of the representation of the kitten.

In terms of the different text types distinguished above, this would seem to be an instructional text, its purpose being to teach the linguistically appropriate way of categorizing objects in the world. As might be expected, therefore, the mode in which mother and child engage with the text is predominantly informational. At the same time, there is also a concern on the mother's part to ensure that Hannah can engage with the text performatively in the sense of being able to "read" the picture.

My third example involves a somewhat older child. David (age three) has chosen a picture storybook called *The Giant Jam Sandwich*, which his mother has had read to him several times before. In the story, a swarm of wasps descends on the town of Itching Down and the inhabitants try, by various means, to get rid of the attacking horde.

M: (reads) 'They drove the picknickers away,
They chased the farmers from their hay.
They stung Lord Swell on his fat bald —'

D: Pate

M: D'you know what a pate is?

D: What?

M: What d'you think it is?

D: Hair

M: Well — yes. It's where his hair SHOULD be. It's his head — look, his bald head. All his hair's gone.

D: Where is it?

M: Well, he's old, so it's dropped out. He's gone bald.

After a little more of the text has been read, David's attention is taken by a picture in which three male inhabitants of Itching Down can be seen, each trying in his own way to fight off the wasps.

D: Is that a spray to shoo them away?

M: Yes. It's probably some sort of insecticide . to get rid of them. And what's that net for, do you think? [Points to a butterfly net]

D: It's for catching them with.

M: It doesn't seem to be much good though, does it?

D: No. They come out the holes.

M: [laughs] The holes are too big, aren't they?
And what about this man? What's he got?

D: He's — What's he got? [The man is wielding a fly swat]

M: What's that?

D: A note. What does the note say?

M: A note on a stick, is it? Is that what you think?

D: Actually it's a sound.

M: A what?

D: A sound. What's it called on the stick? What is it?
What's that man got?

M: Well you know — um —

D: Yes . . . Sign

M: You think it's a sign? Yes it looks very LIKE a sign with writing on, doesn't it?

D: Yes.

M: But it isn't. It's like Mummy's um — fish slice [That is, a slotted spatula]

D: What is it?

M: It's a swatter. He's going to hit the wasp with it. (Wells 1986, pp. 153–4)

In its combination of words and pictures, this composite text has certain similarities with the one that Hannah and her mother were reading. However, there are two important differences. First, the words here form a sustained text that is self-contextualizing; although they certainly complement the written text and add an extra dimension of detail to it, the pictures are not necessary for its interpretation. Second, the purpose of this text is not to instruct but to delight; words and pictures together create an imaginary world that the reader is invited to enter and explore. In terms of the different text types, then, this is an example of literature — a "real" book.

To describe the dominant mode of engagement that is enacted here, by contrast, is much more difficult. In the course of the whole event from which these two episodes have been extracted, David and his mother engage with the text from a variety of points of view. David's first response is affective, as he expresses his dislike of wasps; later, he is concerned about the harm they might cause. In the first episode quoted here, there is also evidence of an informational mode of engagement, as David completes the line of verse with the word "pate," and his mother goes on to explore and extend his understanding of its meaning. In the second episode, it is David's "reading" of the picture that is at issue; he appears to think that the man is holding a written sign telling the wasps to go away. His mother helps him to clarify this interpretation over several turns, expressing appreciation of its plausibility, before finally offering her own, adult, interpretation. To characterize this as an instance of epistemic engagement may be to make too strong a claim. However, in the talk in which they savor and explore the imaginary world created through the words and pictures, David is being helped to construct and evaluate alternative interpretations in a way that is at least incipiently epistemic as well as very clearly re-creational.

In presenting these three examples, it is the differences between them that I have so far tended to emphasize. And these are important. For although in none of them is the text engaged with in only one mode, there is a strong tendency for a particular mode to dominate according to the type of text involved. This was Sulzby and Teale's conclusion, too, based on a much more systematic sampling of shared book readings: even within this much narrower range of text types, they found that "characteristic patterns of reading interaction [were] associated with different types of text" (1987, p. 61). If children are to be introduced to the full potential of literacy, therefore, it is important that they should participate in a wide range of literacy events so that they meet texts of different types and learn how to engage with them appropriately. However, if, as I have suggested, it is the epistemic mode of engagement that most fully exploits the potential of texts for the empowerment of thinking, opportunities should be found for shared literacy events in which the texts involved are likely to elicit this mode of engagement. In the pre-school years, it seems this is most likely to occur in the context of shared storybook reading.

The three examples also share some important similarities, however. For, despite the differences in the types of text involved, the talk between mother and child enacts appropriate ways of engaging with the particular text, thus providing an opportunity for learning about how to engage with a text of that type. In each case, too, the child is encouraged to be an active participant in the event and has his or her contributions as composer or interpreter of the text validated by the adult's acceptance and support. How important these features are can be seen more clearly when they are compared with those that characterize the events through which the literacy curriculum is predominantly enacted in a substantial proportion of primary classrooms (Heap 1985).

Consider the following episode from a session in which the teacher is reading to a group of five-year-olds. The picture storybook, *Little Black Sambo*, has been read without interruptions. The extract below is taken from the talk that immediately follows the reading.[19]

T: What did the first tiger take off Little Black Sambo?

C1: Shirt

(T does not respond)

C2: His coat

T: His coat that his mummy had made
       Do you remember when his mummy made it — what colour was it?

Cs: Red

T: Red, yes .. What did the second tiger take?

Cs: Trousers

T: His trousers .. What did the third tiger take?

Cs: Shoes

T: Was he pleased to take the shoes?

Cs: Yes ·

Cs: No

T: Why not?

C1: Because he had forty feet

T: He said — what did he say to him?

C2: I've got four feet and you've * *

T: I've got four feet and you've got — ?

Cs: Two

T: You haven't got enough shoes for me (Wells 1985b, p. 114)

After more talk of the same kind, the children moved on to another activity.

There are two points that I want to make about this episode by way of contrast with the three preceding examples. The first concerns the impoverished model of literacy that is enacted in the limited — and limiting — question-and-answer sequence that is the only mode in which the teacher draws the children into engaging with the text. Even the "why" question that the teacher asks is not a genuine request for an inference on the children's part, as the reason for the third tiger's dissatisfaction with the shoes is given in the text itself. Thus, by treating the text solely as a series of items of information to be correctly recalled, the teacher reduces this picture storybook to an instructional text, thereby excluding any possibility of the sort of affective and exploratory talk that was so central a feature of David and his mother's discussion of the book they were reading. Second, and as a direct consequence, there is no sense of collaboration. The children dutifully conform to the teacher's agenda but, given no opportunity to express their own reactions to the story, they provide no evidence on the basis of which the teacher could assess the growing edge of their understanding and work with them to extend it through "guided participation".

Unfortunately, despite the spread of the whole language philosophy in the teaching of language arts and the increasing use of children's literature as the basis for the reading program, such instances of missed opportunities are still all too common. Indeed, according to some observers, the testing of "factual" comprehension constitutes the dominant mode of talk about text, whatever the type of text that is being read (Durkin 1979). Nor, in many cases, are the texts children themselves produce made the opportunity for collaborative talk that extends their grasp either of the content or the medium of expression. Unlike the "home" examples discussed above, the talk that occurs tends to be confined to just two modes: the informational and the performative that is needed to support it.

Some would argue that it is the conditions of the classroom that constrain what can be achieved: the externally imposed requirement on teachers to cover the curriculum in the limited time available, which leads to their unwillingness to allow time for the serious consideration of students' points of view, or the perceived impossibility of responding individually to the number of students for whom they are responsible. Others see the problem to be in the students themselves. Their backgrounds and previous experience, it is thought, have not equipped them to be active, independent constructors of meaning who can, with guidance and support, engage with texts in the epistemic mode. This view is often linked to a conviction that students will only be capable of literate thinking when, having been instructed in a predetermined sequence of skill-building exercises, they have mastered all the prerequisite component skills. Whatever the reason, however, the fact of the matter is that, in a substantial proportion of classrooms — at all grade levels — texts are rarely treated as an invitation to discuss alternative possibilities of interpretation or expression, and so students have little opportunity to discover, through such collaborative talk, how an epistemic engagement with text can be a powerful means of achieving understanding.

More and more, however, teachers are discovering that there *are* viable alternatives to a transmission-oriented curriculum. Trusting in their students' disposition actively to make sense of their experience, and reconceptualizing the teaching-learning relationship in terms of transaction rather than transmission, they have found that much more can be achieved in their classrooms than they would originally have believed possible. In the following section, I will present examples taken from the work of two such teachers to illustrate a variety of collaborative activities in which talk about texts provides a much wider range of opportunities for learning to be literate. These examples are taken from observations made in the course of the longitudinal study of language and learning that was described in chapter 1, which also has provided most of the examples discussed in the preceding chapters.

Preparing a Group Presentation

The following episode is taken from a unit of work carried out in Helen Whaley's grade six classroom, in which the students, working in groups organized in terms of reading level, have been studying novels. As the culmination of the unit, each group is to make a presentation to the rest of the class that will give their peers some appreciation of the novel that they have read. The form of the presentation is a matter for each group to decide, the only constraint being that it should involve both oral and written modes of language use. In practice, most groups have decided to include a dramatization of an episode from the novel, written texts that might have been written by characters in the novel, a collage of illustrations with explanatory written text, and some form of oral commentary. The following extracts are taken from a complete morning session during which the groups were reviewing their material in preparation for the final presentations.

The session started with a whole class discussion of the order in which the parts of each group's presentation would be given. This led to the suggestion of producing a written program, the purpose of which was agreed to be that of "preparing [the] audience for what's coming." Then, with the teacher acting as chair and recorder of decisions, the class went on to consider the criteria to be used in evaluating their current drafts. Viewed from the perspective of literacy learning, this reviewing process had the function of encouraging the students to ask themselves questions that required them to adopt a variety of orientations to the texts they had created: Were they organized in such a way as to be effective in conveying a sense of the novel studied (functional)? Were they conventionally presented in terms of spelling, punctuation, etc. (performative)? Was the information they contained accurate (informational)?

As the discussion proceeded, various components of the presentations were considered, with the students making suggestions as to how they should be evaluated, which the teacher wrote on the board. Central to these was the criterion implied by Nadir's question: "Does it make sense?" It was in considering the picture collages from this point of view that the teacher was led to introduce a further important criterion that had not yet been explicitly mentioned.

T: Yes I'm glad you mentioned this because I'd almost forgotten it but I went back Friday night and I was reading some of those things . .
Make sure your text explains your picture . .
Remember twenty-four of us have not read your text . . . . .
You see you haven't helped me as a reader, if you don't give me a little guidance . .

This is important [writes] 'Text and picture — what kind of information are you really giving?'
I think everybody needs to take a look at that to make sure you are telling us something significant

Here, as in the discussion of the written program that it was agreed each group should prepare, the teacher makes explicit the need to think of their presentations as communications to an audience. Their texts do not exist in a void, but in a particular social context, they are intended to be informative for their peers, who have not read the novels being discussed. Although this is implicitly understood by the students, it is apparently not sufficiently well established as one of their text production strategies for any one of them to have suggested this criterion spontaneously in the course of the discussion. By talking about it explicitly, however, the teacher tries to make it more likely that they will make use of this criterion as they check their texts in preparation for the presentations.

By emphasizing the necessity of taking account of the needs of the audience, the teacher has nudged the class in the direction of adopting an overall epistemic orientation to the texts they have produced. For what she is asking them to do is to review their texts from a different perspective — that of a reader or listener who is not familiar with the novel in question. To decide whether their texts are effective, therefore, they must ask themselves not only whether the information is accurate, but also whether it is selected and presented in a way that makes it interesting and intelligible to the audience for whom it is intended. Put more abstractly, she is asking them to think of composing as involving an interaction between the two essential goals of selecting appropriate content and of shaping and expressing it to achieve a particular rhetorical purpose (Scardamalia and Bereiter 1985). To approach the evaluation task in this way will certainly require them to engage with their texts in the epistemic mode. In the first part of the session, then, a set of criteria is constructed for the groups to use in evaluating and revising their material, which requires the students to adopt all five modes of engagement in reviewing the texts they have prepared.

What is equally important to note, however, is the collaborative manner in which this is done. Throughout the discussion, the teacher makes it clear that the responsibility for the form a group's presentation takes rests with the students: "It's your right to prepare your programme whatever way you so desire as long as it achieves your purpose. 'What is the purpose of your program?' — that's what you have to keep in mind." The validity of the students' ideas is also emphasized in the compilation of the set of criteria to be used in reviewing the different types of text they have produced. However, in introducing and explaining a criterion that the students, on their own, had not suggested, the teacher also contributes to the discussion from her own greater expertise as a writer.

Viewed in terms of the Vygotskian framework introduced above, the whole episode can be seen as an example of teaching as "assisting the learners' performance." The teacher starts by establishing what the students can do alone and then, on that basis, moves the talk into what she judges to be their "zone of proximal development." The complete list of criteria that results is thus a joint production, but one that goes beyond what the students could have produced on their own. As she brings this part of the session to a close, the teacher underlines both the epistemic stance the students need to adopt to their texts and her conception of learning through collaborative activity:

> You've got your pictures and you've got your idea of who you want to explain it to. Now the next step is just to revise. Add more if you need to add more, take away this if you don't need it. And as a group you help each other do that 'cos sometimes seven pairs of eyes can see things that one pair can't.

Solving a Problem Together

Immediately after this whole-class session, the students went to work in their groups. Within minutes, there was evidence that at least one group — Danny, Julie, Govinda, Phuong, Nadir, Mink, and Andrew — was attempting to put into practice the criteria that had been agreed upon, when its members asked the teacher to help them resolve a problem that had arisen.

As already mentioned, one of the types of text that several groups had decided to produce was a collage in which pictures, cut from magazines to illustrate characters and events in the novel, were accompanied by some form of explanatory written text. In fact, it was these explanatory captions that the teacher was referring to, in particular, when she asked the students to make sure they were "saying something significant." In the group that the teacher has joined, more than one of these collages has been produced and the problem is that, because they were not produced in collaboration, there are both discrepancies and redundancies between them. The teacher suggests, therefore, that they look at each collage in turn to establish how it contributes to the total presentation.

They start with Julie's collage, and the teacher asks her to explain: "Julie tell us what you think you've got here .. what you're aiming for." With some prompting by other members of the group and by the teacher, Julie identifies three categories of picture: people, places, and equipment that figure prominently in the novel. It is in relation to a picture in this latter category that the following episode occurs. In it, the teacher extends the earlier discussion by operationalizing one particular way in which a text can be examined to see if it achieves the author's purpose.

T: There's one question I have . What kind of skis are these?

J: I don't know (softly)
[Children lean forward to look more closely. Several suggestions are made, all of them inaudible]

T: For use on what or in what conditions?

G: For — ground

S: _*_ mountains

P: Er — downhill ski

Ss: Yes

T: Are they?

J: No I don't think so

N: Slalom

G: Cross-country?

M: No mountain skis . downhill
[Several speak at once]

T: OK I can see — How many of you people here have ever water skied?

A: Those are water skis?

D: <u>Those are</u> water skis?

T: Those are water skis

?: * * * *

Ss: Oh yeah

T: If you've never water-skied you might not pick this up [Several laugh] But you were right when you said slalom but they're slalom water-skis . er — they have a totally different . er — size and um [Ss laugh] and er — binding . but because you have never water-skied you didn't pick that up
I have here somewhere in our books a whole bunch of winter . skiing . er — magazines . where you can get pictures of winter skis

J: I think we saw that <u>book</u>

T: <u>You</u> probably saw it . I think this is a marvellous idea to have a ski . picture . but let's make sure we get skis for winter conditions

What has happened here is that the teacher has picked up a mismatch between the type of skis illustrated in the picture Julie had selected for her collage and the type of skis that figured in the novel, and she has drawn the group's attention to it as a discrepancy. The text the student has created is not an accurate representation of the novel text from which they started. From this point of view, it does not "make sense"; revision of a particular kind is needed.

Although in itself this incident may seem to concern no more than an isolated detail, in what follows it becomes clear that the teacher has provided a demonstration of a more generally applicable strategy for evaluating their texts in a way that enables the students to appropriate it and put it to use for themselves. For, immediately after this sequence, Danny makes an objection to another picture, pointing out that "It's supposed to be snowing — and it's summer" (referring to the background in the picture), and they discuss various ways of overcoming the problem. "Excellent suggestion," comments the teacher. "Then you get rid of this conflicting information." This is followed by a further instance, also initiated by a student and, finally by the following discussion, in which the task of matching a picture to an aspect of the novel is seen to be, not an absolute matter, but one involving judgment of quite a complex kind.

This discussion starts with Phuong pointing to another pictorial representation, which she considers to be discrepant, since the dog in the picture does not look like her personal representation of the dog, Arthur, in the novel. However, as Julie points out, in defense of her choice, "It's hard to find a dog that's Arthur." Some of the other students agree, and the teacher, perhaps conscious that Julie, as the creator of the collage that has provided the material for this collaborative evaluation, has had to accept a considerable amount of implied criticism, introduces the important pragmatic consideration that if one attempts to be too precise, one may find oneself unable to proceed.

T: You've really got a choice . if you can't find a picture of that kind of dog . then are you saying don't use any dog at all or use a dog and say this represents Arthur?

A: * choose a dog that represents Arthur

P: Don't use a . dog

G: Use a dog.

T: Is Arthur important to the story?

J, G, A, & M: (in chorus) Yes

D & L: (in chorus) No

J, G, A, & M: (in chorus) Yeah

D: What did he do?

P: He ran away

J: He got . he got — he came back with the people . remember?

G: Yeah . He — he helped them out of the tunnel . *

A & N: Yeah

A: Remember when he was trapped in the tunnel * * *
[Several speak at once]

A: * * out then he followed Arthur all the way round and <dragged> him out

G: Yeah

N: yeah
[Several speak at once in agreement]

T: I've got another question . How is it they got lost?

A: Arthur

N: Arthur

T: Is Arthur important?

A, N, & G: Yeah

T: OK

With the question about Arthur's importance to the story, the talk moves to a new level of sophistication. For, in order to answer it, the students are forced to reinterrogate their mental representations of the whole novel and to compare their judgments of the significance of particular events in order to decide how important a role Arthur plays. This is indeed to engage with the text of the novel in the epistemic mode. With the final, unopposed, decision that Arthur is indeed important, the matter of the appropriateness of the pictorial representation is also implicitly resolved and Julie's choice is vindicated.

The episodes we have just examined all occurred in one phase of a larger project, the purpose of which was, in the teacher's words, "to show that you have understood what you have read by explaining the story" through different forms of re-presentation. But "showing what you have understood" is not self-explanatory. What does it mean to have understood a story? And how do you know when you have successfully shown that understanding? By engaging with the students in collaborative talk about the texts that they had read and those that they were creating, the teacher was able to help them extend the criteria for evaluating their understanding and their success in representing it; she was also able to involve them in a joint enactment of some of the relevant strategies.

Winter and the Yukon

The second of my examples comes from the project on winter and the Yukon, which was described in chapters 3 and 4. As will be recalled, Ann Maher, the teacher of the combined grade three and four class, decided to launch the theme of winter by reading Robert Service's ballad, "The Cremation of Sam McGee." Following the first reading of the poem the children worked in self-chosen groups, creating models of various kinds to advertise the newly illustrated edition of the poem. The group that I observed in detail used an enormous cardboard carton to make a model bookstore with a large window in which many miniature books were displayed, together with posters advertising the new book. Another group made a model of the ship's boiler in which Sam McGee was cremated, with a pop-up figure of McGee speaking from amidst the flames.

On the third day, the teacher read the ballad to the class again and then, in a half-hour brainstorming session, invited the children to think of questions arising from the poem to which they would like to find answers. Many questions were suggested concerning the geography of the Yukon, who discovered it, its climate, its flora and fauna, and so on. Then, when the teacher had spent a few minutes showing the children how their questions fell into groups corresponding to the disciplines known as history, geography, etc., she asked them each to choose the question they wished to tackle and who they would like to work with, to sign up with their topics on the sheet she had provided, and to start work. She announced that she would talk with each group as soon as they had worked out what they wanted to do.

The task for each group, therefore, was to carry out research on their chosen topic and to find some way of representing what they discovered so that it could be shared with other people; the final outcome of their work was to be the presentation of their projects at a parents' open house evening several weeks later. Written texts were certainly included in the types of outcome the teacher expected, but she encouraged them to explore other modes of representation, such as models and diagrams. One girl even produced a tape-recorded set of instructions on how to perform a simple experiment she had set up to show how wind is the result of convection currents created by the heat from the sun (see chapter 4 pp. 88−89).

Long before one begins to think about the final mode of textual presentation, however, the first problem to be solved is that of defining one's topic or, in the case of an inquiry-based project, of identifying the question to be researched. For nine- and ten-year-olds this may be a challenge not encountered before — as it was for Brian and Kim, two nine-year-old Chinese-Canadian students. And when one is still learning the language of the classroom, as they were, the challenge is even more daunting. Aware of their probable difficulty, therefore, the teacher does not wait for them to come to her but calls them for a conference to help them find a topic. "Do you want to come here and think about what projects you're going to work on?" she asks. "What really interests YOU? Things about the animals, the people?"

How do you know which questions you would be interested in researching? What is research, anyway? And where do you find researchable questions? Couched in the language of the classroom, these are questions to which the two boys' previous experience provides no answers. Of course, they have discovered a great deal that has interested them by observing, experimenting, and asking questions about the objects and events that they have incidentally encountered in their homes and community. But it is a very different matter to be asked deliberately to choose a topic to work on in the more formal, text-oriented context of the classroom. Initially, then, the two boys can think of nothing to say in response to the teacher's question.

The teacher, on the other hand, believes on the basis of past experience that most questions become interesting once one has made a commitment to trying to find answers to them. However, she also knows that enthusiasm is more likely to develop if the question can grow out of an existing interest. Her first problem, therefore, is to find a point of departure. Brian has already written down one or two questions that provide some possible leads, but he does not seem to be particularly enthusiastic about any of them. For his part, Kim has so far expressed no ideas at all. As they are considering the possibility of studying the history of the Yukon (the teacher's gloss on one of Brian's questions), she remembers seeing Brian looking at an atlas. "You're interested in maps, too, aren't you Brian?" she asks, and he nods in agreement. "I wonder if there's some way you could work on the map of the Yukon too—d'you think that would fit into your question?" At that point, Kim asks about Tennessee (the original home of Sam McGee) and the teacher, seeing a possible starting point, suggests that they fetch the globe and try to locate Tennessee and the Yukon.

Some minutes later, after the boys have had a chance to explore the globe, the teacher rejoins them and, together, they look for Yukon and Tennessee and note the distance between them. Looking further afield, the boys notice with surprise how small Britain is and they talk some more about other countries, their size and the distances between them. Finally, the teacher, who has been answering another child's question, turns back to them and tries to move them towards a decision:

T: OK I want to talk to you two .
    Now you've spent . a lot of time looking at the globe haven't you? . .
    You look both very interested in maps . I wonder . if you could try . and draw a map as part of your project?
    Would that interest you?
[B and K look dubious]

T: You could do * *

B: Too hard

T: For you? Well how about—

B: Tracing?

T: Tracing?   .   Pretty small that's the only trouble isn't it?
[Two inaudible utterances]

T: Would you feel brave enough to try to DRAW one to make it larger?
    You could just use a scrap of paper and try it out . do a rough copy to see how it works
    You never know . it might work * * * Want to try a rough copy?

B: (still somewhat reluctant) <I don't know>

T: Well who's going to know if you don't know?
    How about you Kim? Do you want to try?

K: * * * *

T: It's a good idea to try it out
    If you want to go to the cupboard and just take a piece of . you know the big paper . the newsprint . just for a rough copy . OK? and see how it works out . If you don't try it you'll never know

B: OK

Did they jump or were they pushed? Probably a bit of each; for, despite their apparent interest in maps, without the teacher's articulation of the first steps to take and her insistence that they give it a try, they might have remained forever on the brink. However, to pose the issue in terms of an either/or question is to misunderstand the essentially collaborative nature of the teaching-learning relationship, as this was explicated by Vygotsky. Left to their own devices, he points out, learners are limited to the competences that they have already acquired. In the present instance, for Brian and Kim, these skills did not include being able to choose a topic they would be interested in exploring. The role of the teacher, therefore, is to engage with the learner in a task that is slightly beyond his or her current capability and, by "assisting his performance" in that task, to "awaken and rouse to life those functions which are in a state of maturing or in the zone of proximal development" (Vygotsky 1956, p. 278, quoted in Wertsch and Stone 1985). Viewed in this way, the choice of maps as a topic to be explored is a shared achievement and one that, with further such collaborative experiences, Brian and Kim will be able to undertake on their own.

The appropriateness of this analysis of the episode just described is borne out by what followed. Having been helped to get launched into their project, the two boys became fully involved. First, they succeeded in drawing a very creditable map of Canada, on which they marked the Yukon and some of the major cities. Then they went on each to create a board game, based on the knowledge they had gained, in which players advanced their pieces according to their ability to answer questions correctly about Canadian geography.

Two weeks later, as the groups were completing their projects, the teacher met with Brian and Kim again to discuss the form their final presentation would take. By this stage, the group included another Asian boy, Luke, who had joined them shortly after the episode described in the previous paragraphs. Having negotiated what remains to be done, the teacher suggests that Kim might like to write about how they came to carry out the project and this leads to the following retrospective review:

T: Remember we talked—that you—Yes I think it was Kim and Brian . remember the first day or two we were talking about making maps and things . and Luke got <u>interested</u>

B: <u>Oh I</u> remember

T: Do you remember?

B: Yes and Luke asked

T: Luke asked?

B: Yes

T: What did he ask?

B: Asked could he join our group to make maps

T: Oh and he wanted to join the group?

B: <u>Yeh</u>

T: D'<u>you</u> remember that Luke . right . and you started to make maps?

B: Yeh

T: Remember how you started? What did you do first?

B: Well we started the <dots> . on the —

L: No not that

T: Oooh (expressing great interest)

L: That was the second

T: Was that the second? Following the dots . that was on the —

B: First you told us to try and make one (=a map)

T: Yeh oh I remember . <u>you</u> —

B: <u>And the</u> — and the other day — day . you got the other map for us

T: Oh yes, that big <u>one</u>

B: <u>This</u> one (pointing to the large atlas)

T: [Answers a question asked by another student]
Right . and you got the big one and then you <u>traced the</u> —

B: <u>And you told us to trace from dots</u>

T: <u>You're right about the dots I remember</u>
So that you know which province was which

L: Then we traced it over then we got this map (i.e. the large one that they are going to display with their games)

T: And then you got the big map uh-huh

L: Yeh

T: And then what did you do?

B: And somebody got the idea of making a game

T: Yeh I don't know where that game — that game idea came from . Do you remember? <u>* * *</u>

B: <u>From a magazine</u> * . I think Annie

T: Pardon dear?

B: I think it's Annie's

T: Oh I remember we were sitting together in a group and we were thinking about how we could finish projects

B: And then the <pattern> Luke want to make a game and I said "No . takes lots of time".

T: <u>(laughs)</u>

B: — and I think it all over that I made it . then we decided to make a map game

T: Yeah yeh . so that's how your project — you changed your ideas and it sort of grew didn't it. with all your ideas?

B: Yeh

In this conversation, the evolution of the finished texts — map and board games — is reconstructed so that the boys can see how their ideas originated and developed. By getting them to talk about the process involved, the teacher brings these processes to their level of conscious awareness so that they can reflect upon what they have been doing. In the light of their initial uncertainty and reluctance to commit themselves, some important points emerge:

1. It is not necessary to have a fully worked-out idea of the end point in order to get started.

2. New ideas present themselves as one works on one's material, some of which may be worth developing further.

3. Revision of one's goals, as well as of the actual text, is a normal and important part of carrying out any project.

4. A topic often becomes more interesting the more one works on it.

During the same two weeks, the teacher talked with the other groups, giving each the assistance that she judged most relevant to the topics they had chosen and their ability to handle them. The final outcomes of their projects varied considerably in quality, of course, as might be expected in a class differing so much in age and previous experience. However, through the activities involved in carrying out their projects, and through the conferences they had with their teacher, each child encountered important principles about learning through inquiry. And what was most important, those principles were encountered, not in an abstract lecture, but in their enactment in joint activity and in the talk that accompanied it.

Shortly after the parents' evening, at which the children presented their projects and answered questions about what they had been doing, I met with Maher, the teacher, to review the material I had collected. As we looked at the video recordings I had made of the class at work, and at the transcripts of her meetings with the different groups, she commented on the similarity between the processes involved in planning and carrying out an inquiry and those involved in composing a written text. In particular, she noted how similar her own role was in facilitating the two processes (see p. 72).

As she had implicitly realized, literacy is essentially the use of texts — that is to say, external representations in a variety of media: models, maps, and even games, as well as written documents — to explore and develop ideas, to record what one has come to know, and to represent that knowledge in a form that is interesting and useful to others. It was this power of texts — of all kinds — as tools for thinking, learning, and communicating that she was helping the children to discover as she provided experiences over the year in which reading, writing, doing, thinking, and talking were brought to bear on topics that they found interesting and challenging. And, as a result, they became engaged in activities that, at a level appropriate to their ability, involved them, at critical moments, in adopting an epistemic stance to the texts that they were creating.[20]

However, just as important for the children's development as literate thinkers was Maher's awareness of her own critical role in this process, both in creating the context for their inquiries, and also in encouraging the children to engage in collaborative talk with herself as teacher and also with each other about the functional significance of the various texts they were using and creating. As the examples I have quoted here and in earlier chapters show, it was through this exploratory and reflective talk that they were learning the potential that texts have to contribute to the achievement of understanding.

Teachers as Learners

In the previous two sections, I have presented examples of classrooms in which talk about texts provided opportunities for students to appropriate the inner, invisible mental activities that are at the heart of literacy. Because these activities are not apparent in the surface behavior of a person who is engaging with a text, they are more appropriately made available to learners through talk about activities in which the learner is also engaged as a partner in the collaborative enterprise. This is what is meant by describing learning in school as an "intellectual apprenticeship," in which students are drawn into the practices and modes of discourse of the various discipline-based communities of scholars that are valued in the culture and, through assisted performance, enabled to appropriate those practices and modes of discourse and make them their own.

The two teachers from whose classrooms these examples were taken showed in their practice that, implicitly at least, they understood and shared the theory of literacy and learning that I have attempted to present in this chapter. However, there are still many teachers whose practice is based on quite different principles. In their classrooms, a rather limited conception of literacy seems to underlie the activities that students undertake, and talk tends to be organized around the *transmission and assessment* of information rather than as a medium for collaboration in the *transactional construction* of understanding. As a result, students often fail to display their full potential, and the shortcomings in their performance are attributed to inadequacies in their home and community backgrounds or to their own limited abilities, rather than to the absence of challenging and engaging opportunities to make sense of new ideas and events in the activities that are provided for them in the classroom.

The question, then, is how to persuade these teachers to create, in their classrooms, communities of active inquirers, who exploit the full potential of literacy to empower their learning. Or, in more general terms, how does one bring about educational change in schools? It is to a consideration of this question that I wish to turn in the final section of this chapter.

The first point to emphasize is that, if the principles of learning that have been set out above are valid, they apply to teachers as much as they do to children. Indeed, it is doubly important, if teachers are to learn to apply these principles in their curriculum planning and in its enactment, that they experience those same principles in action in their own continuing education. If there is to be a change in classroom practices, therefore, it cannot be brought about in a mechanical way, but must be the result of a change in teachers' ways of thinking about their role in relation to their students' learning. This conclusion is amply demonstrated in recent research on implementing educational change, which has shown that where educational innovation is imposed from above without teacher participation at the stages of selecting the changes to be made and planning the means of implementation, the desired changes are at best short-lived and at worst subtly but systematically rejected (Fullan 1982). The only effective way of bringing about educational change, therefore, as Stenhouse (1975) argued, is through the professional development of teachers.

Until recently, two basic approaches have been taken to further professional development. In the first, the emphasis has been placed on practice. According to those who advocate this approach, what matters most is that teachers should behave in the "correct" ways, and so, through training courses, practical workshops, and demonstrations, attempts have been made to modify actual teaching behaviors. In the second approach, the emphasis has been placed on theory, on the grounds that only when teachers hold appropriate beliefs, will they modify their practice in the desired manner. Both approaches, however, have failed to bring about the desired changes.

The reasons for the ineffectiveness of the first approach have already been suggested. New modes of behavior are not incorporated into existing repertoires unless the patterns to be learned are perceived to be functional, meaningful, and relevant. That is to say, they must grow out of the teacher's evaluation of a situation as problematic and in need of change. Furthermore, the proposed change must be grounded in theory. To that extent, the proponents of the second approach are correct in placing an emphasis on theory. But theory that does not grow out of firsthand experience may all too easily remain inert and so have no effect in bringing about change in practice. What is needed, therefore, is an approach to teachers' further professional development that recognizes, first, that learning is a matter of individual, cumulative construction and must therefore be based on each teacher's current understanding and, second, that theory and practice stand in a dialectical relationship to each other, each influencing and being influenced by the other. The implication of these principles is that the most effective professional development will be classroom based and problem oriented. It should also be conducted in ways that encourage collaboration among colleagues, both within and between institutions. In other words, the emphasis will be on enabling teachers to acquire the competences and resources to be systematic and intentional learners in and about their own professional situations and the confidence and disposition to use them (Duckworth 1987; Connelly and Chandinin 1988).

In the last few years, a variety of new approaches have been adopted that attempt to meet these conditions, under such titles as "classroom inquiry," "teacher as researcher," "collaborative action research" (e.g., Goswami and Stillman 1987; Pinnell and Matlin 1989). What all have in common is the recognition of the importance of treating the teacher as an agent with respect to her or his own learning, while at the same time providing some form of professional support. In the following paragraphs I should like to describe one approach that has grown out of our work on the development of literacy. Indeed, as I shall try to show, this approach is in itself an exemplification of how understanding is empowered through an epistemic engagement with text. To make this connection, however, I shall need to extend somewhat further the definition of text that has been developed in the preceding pages.

A written text, it has been argued, functions as a cognitive amplifier (Bruner 1972) in providing an external and fixed representation of the outcome of intentional mental processes, which can be read, reflected upon, revised, and rewritten. In the process, the writer's understanding of the topic may be significantly enhanced, as may be that of other readers, if they share the cultural conventions that enable them to construct an interpretation. On the same basis, as has already been argued, orally produced texts, if they are recorded or recalled verbatim, and other forms of symbolic representation, such as models, paintings, and films, can perform a similar function. And so, by a further extension, can audio and video recordings of classroom activities, when they are treated as texts that may be interpreted, reflected upon, and made the basis for revised classroom practice.

The recognition of the potential of video recordings to function in this way as reflective texts emerged gradually from a number of classroom inquiries in which researchers collaborated with interested teachers on topics that arose during our longitudinal study. Indeed, each of the teachers from whose classrooms the preceding examples were taken was involved in such an inquiry. Overall, the topics that were addressed varied quite widely. In one school, for example, they ranged from a comparison of different ways of organizing opportunities for children to engage in learning cooperatively, through an exploration of ways of integrating reading and writing with a practical study of energy, to an investigation of the advantages and disadvantages of different ways of giving feedback to children on their writing. Just as the topics varied, so did the teachers' reasons for addressing them. In some cases, the impetus came from outside the classroom — a suggestion or recommendation from a consultant or a workshop leader to try a pedagogical technique new to the teacher concerned. In other cases, the impetus came from the teacher's reflection on her or his own teaching: a specific question was formulated and methods of data collection and analysis were designed to answer the question.

In every case, however, video recordings of the children, as they carried out the various activities that the teachers had arranged, provided one essential component. After both teacher and researcher had viewed the tapes independently, a meeting was held at which selected extracts were reviewed together. Under these conditions, with the opportunity they provided for alternative interpretations to be considered and the evidence for them to be critically examined, the recordings, instead of simply providing a narrative-like account to be viewed relatively uncritically, functioned as both a source of evidence for answering the teacher's original question and as a stimulus to reflection and further inquiry. They thus became texts of classroom practice, which teachers and researchers talked about collaboratively in order to plan and evaluate revisions in the provision of learning opportunities for students.[21]

Over and over again in reviewing these texts, what impressed the teachers were the abilities their children demonstrated, their sustained involvement in an activity when it was personally meaningful to them, their willingness to ask questions of each other and give critical consideration to suggested answers, and their concern to produce a finished product that would be successful in communicating to their intended audience. Faced with this evidence, the teachers found themselves having to reconsider some of the assumptions on which they based their pedagogical decisions. Beliefs that had before been tacit became more explicit and, in some cases, were found to need radical change.

For many of the teachers, the expectation that they would present the results of their inquiries to a wider audience was a significant factor in the total experience, particularly when this led to the preparation of a written script. Aware of the demands for explicitness and systematicity of exposition that are placed on a writer by the anticipated needs of the audience, they were forced to take the processes that had begun in discussion a stage further, as they tried, through reflection, further reading, writing, and revising to make their personal connections between theory and practice clearer for themselves so that they could make them clear for their readers and listeners.

In effect, what was happening was that the teachers were engaging with texts, both written and video-recorded, in the same sort of critical and creative way that I have been advocating for younger learners. And the results were doubly beneficial — as they themselves recognized. First, they were better able to see how, for reading and writing to contribute to learning, the task that provides the context for these activities must be meaningful and relevant to the students; it must also be one that challenges them to engage with the text epistemically. Second, they began to discover how their own involvement in a classroom-based inquiry could function as a demonstration to their students of the very same behaviors they wanted them to learn. And, as always, it was talk with their colleagues and researcher collaborators that helped them to discover the personal significance of the texts on which they were working.

Conclusion

In the examples presented and discussed in the preceding pages, I have tried to show that literacy is not a single, homogeneous competence, but that instead it involves being able to engage with texts of different types in modes appropriate to the different purposes people have in using them. In particular, I have emphasized the powerful role that texts can play in intellectual development when they are engaged with epistemically as an external representation of meaning that can be reflected upon, interrogated, and revised. To learn how to engage with texts in ways appropriate to the purposes they can serve, however, children need to see and hear enactments of those inner mental processes that are the essence of literate behavior so that they can appropriate them and deploy them for themselves. And it is through collaborative talk about texts of varying kinds in the context of meaningful joint activities, undertaken with the assistance of a more skilled co-participant, I have argued, that this learning can most effectively occur. It is in this sense, I have suggested, that learning to be literate can be thought of as an intellectual apprenticeship.

If children are to have opportunities to learn in this way, however, there will need to be radical changes in the ways in which most teachers think about the place of texts of various kinds in their classroom programs and about their own role in helping children to engage with them appropriately. For this to happen, I have argued, teachers need to become learners about literacy and learning through the same sort of processes of inquiry, conducted in their own classrooms, as those that have been advocated for the children that they teach. One such mode of professional development, which has been found valuable by those teachers who have engaged in it, involves the use of video-recorded observations made in their class-rooms over the course of some curricular unit. By treating such recordings as texts, which can be reflected upon through writing and through collaborative talk with colleagues and other educators, teachers have been enabled to learn — in their zones of proximal development — to create classroom communities that provide oppor-tunities to engage in such collaborative talk about texts — communi-ties in which *all* exploit the potential of literacy to empower their thinking, acting, and feeling.

However, since it is the teachers' own words that provide the strongest testimony to the value of this sort of professional develop-ment, I should like to conclude by recalling Maher's reflections on what she learned from the inquiry she carried out on the place of revision in her classroom. As she discovered, revision does not apply only to writing; rather, "it has everything to do with reflecting on plans, and making changes where it seems most reasonable to do so."

Reviewing her inquiry as a whole, she wrote (p. 21):

> As I become a more reflective practitioner, in turn my changing behaviour seems to have a more immediate effect on the children. I am constantly reminded that what the teacher demonstrates with sincerity has the greatest impact. . . .

Although my inquiry is far from complete, my professional behaviour in the classroom has changed as the children and I are drawn more closely together into a community of learners, working to explore, to reflect and, in the light of new information, to revise old assumptions and to expand our understanding of the processes of thinking and learning.

Notes

13. In this context, it is interesting to consider Scribner and Cole's (1981) account of the uses to which the much more recently invented Vai script is put in the lives of those who use it.

14. The present proposal is a revised version of an earlier model that was first presented in Wells (1987).

15. The contrast between the informational and re-creational modes proposed here is somewhat similar to Rosenblatt's distinction between the "efferent" and the "aesthetic" stance in her transactional theory of reading. While the efferent stance is concerned with the information that is carried away from the text, the aesthetic stance she describes as "an attitude of readiness to focus attention on what is being lived through *during* the reading event" (1988, p. 5, original emphasis).

16. This, I think, is very similar to the conclusion reached by Scribner and Cole (1981) on the basis of their study of Vai literacy.

17. Considerable effort has been devoted to the attempt to produce a taxonomy of text types, starting with the classical rhetoricians and continuing to the present day. In recent years, notable contributions have been made by Britton et al. (1975) in their study of secondary students' writing, and by Halliday and his associates at the University of Sydney in the field of genre study (Halliday 1985; Martin 1984; Painter and Martin 1987). However, because such attempts have been motivated by different purposes, they have given rise to a number of alternative taxonomies, none of which is exhaustive or of universal applicability.

18. Since cultures certainly differ from each other in the values they ascribe to different types of text and to the purposes for which they engage with them (Schieffelin 1987), this definition is deliberately couched in terms that allow for alternative interpretations with respect to particular cultures.

19. Although some readers may find the story itself offensive, I have chosen to include this example because it provides a particularly clear example of an approach to reading instruction that is, regrettably, still all too frequent.

20. In this context, it is interesting to read Lampert's (1989) account of the way she teaches fifth graders to solve mathematical problems, which she sees as an example of the 'epistemic teaching of school mathematics'; two features of this approach are the use of multiple modes of representation (or what I have been calling texts in modes other than the written), and dialogues among teacher and learners. Describing a unit on decimals in which she used the segmentation of a circle to represent decimal fractions, she writes, 'I teach students to use representational tools to reason about numerical relationships. In the public discourse of the classroom, such reasoning occurs as argument among peers and between students and teacher. It is the ability to participate in such arguments that is the mark of mathematics learning' (p. 249).

21. Video recordings have, of course, been used before in teacher education, particularly in the period when "micro-teaching" was in vogue. What distinguishes their use in the present situation is the more agentive role given to and taken on by the teachers in deciding what issues to address and what actions to take in the light of their interpretation of the evidence the recordings provided.

References

Anderson, J.R. 1982. "Acquisition of cognitive skill." *Psychological Review*, 89: 369–406.

Apple, M.W. 1990. *Ideology and the curriculum*. Second edition. New York: Routledge.

Atkin, M. 1991. "Teaching as research." Invited address presented at the Annual Conference of the American Educational Research Association, Chicago, 3–7 April 1991.

Atwell, N. 1991. *Side by side: Essays on teaching to learn*. Portsmouth, NH: Heinemann.

———, ed. 1990. *Coming to know: Writing to learn in the intermediate grades*. Portsmouth, NH: Heinemann.

Baird, W. In press. "Literate thinking in the classroom." In W. Baird and G. Wells, *Language and learning: Learners, teachers and researchers at work*. Vol. 1. *Description and evaluation*. Toronto: Ontario Ministry of Education.

Baker, C.D. and P. Freebody. 1989. *Children's first school books*. Oxford: Blackwell.

Bakhtin, M.M. 1981. *The dialogic imagination: Four essays by M.M. Bakhtin*. Austin: University of Texas Press.

———. 1986. *Speech genres and other late essays*. Austin: University of Texas Press.

Barnes, D. 1990. "Language in the secondary classroom." In D. Barnes, J. Britton, and H. Rosen, *Language, the learner and the school*. Portsmouth, NH: Boynton/Cook-Heinemann.

———. 1992. *From communication to curriculum*. Portsmouth, NH: Boynton/Cook-Heinemann.

Beaugrande, R. de. 1984. *Text production: toward a science of composition*. Norwood, NJ: Ablex.

Bereiter, C. 1985. "Toward a solution of the learning paradox." *Review of Educational Research*, 55 (2): 201–26.

Bereiter, C. and M. Scardamalia. 1987. *The psychology of written composition*. Hillsdale, NJ: Lawrence Erlbaum Associates.

———. 1989. "Intentional learning as a goal of instruction." In L.B. Resnick, ed. *Knowing, learning, and instruction: Essays in honor of Robert Glaser*. Hillsdale, NJ: Lawrence Erlbaum Associates.

Bettencourt, A. 1991. On what it means to understand science. Unpublished paper, Michigan State University.

Blake, M. In press. "Collaborative research: teachers as researchers." In M. Blake, G.L. Chang, and G. Wells, eds. 1991. *Language and learning: Learners, teachers and researchers at work*. Volume 4: *Collaborative Research*. Toronto: Ontario Ministry of Education.

Booth, D. and C. Thornley-Hall, eds. 1991. *Classroom talk*. Portsmouth, NH: Heinemann.

Bower, T. 1974. *Development in infancy*. San Francisco: W.H. Freeman.

Britton, J. 1970. *Language and learning*. London: Allen Lane.

Britton, J., T. Burgess, N. Martin, A. McLeod, and H. Rosen. 1975. *The development of writing abilities, 11–18*. London: Macmillan.

Brown, R. 1973. *A first language*. Cambridge: Harvard University Press.

Bruner, J.S. 1972. *The relevance of education*. Harmondsworth, Middlesex: Penguin.

————. 1986. *Actual minds, possible worlds*. Cambridge: Harvard University Press.

Bruner, J.S. and H. Haste, eds. 1987. *Making sense: The child's construction of the world*. London: Methuen.

Camp, G., ed. 1982. *Teaching writing: Essays from the Bay Area Writing Project*. Portsmouth, NH: Boynton/Cook-Heinemann.

Chafe, W. 1985. "Linguistic differences produced by differences between speaking and writing." In D.R. Olson, N. Torrance, and A. Hildyard, eds. *Literacy, language, and learning*. Cambridge: Cambridge University Press.

Chang, G.L. and G. Wells. Forthcoming. "The dynamics of discourse: Literacy and the construction of knowledge." In E. Forman, N. Minick, and A. Stone, eds. *Contexts for learning: Sociocultural dynamics in children's development*. New York: Oxford University Press.

Chang, G.L., et al. 1988. "Improving opportunities for literacy learning through teacher-researcher collaboration: a symposium presented at The International Reading Association in Toronto. In M. Blake, G.L. Chang, and G. Wells, eds. 1991. *Language and learning: Learners, teachers, and researchers at work*. Volume 4: *Collaborative Research*. Toronto: Ontario Ministry of Education.

Cole, M. and J.S. Bruner. 1971. "Cultural differences and inferences about psychological processes." *American Psychologist*, 2: 867–76.

Connelly, E.M. and D.J. Clandinin. 1988. *Teachers as curriculum planners*. Toronto, Ontario: OISE Press.

Corson, D. 1988. *Oral language across the curriculum*. Clevedon, U.K.: Multilingual Matters.

Cross, T.G. 1978. "Mothers' speech and its association with rate of linguistic development in young children." In N. Waterson and C. Snow, eds. *The development of communication*. Chichester, U.K.: Wiley.

Cummins, J. 1984. *Bilingualism and special education: Issues in assessment and pedagogy*. Clevedon, U.K.: Multilingual Matters.

Dewey, J. 1900. *The school and society*. Chicago: University of Chicago Press.

Donaldson, M. 1978. *Children's minds*. London: Fontana.

Driver, R. 1983. *The pupil as scientist?* Milton Keynes, U.K.: Open University Press.

Duckworth, E. 1987. *"The having of wonderful ideas" and other essays on teaching and learning*. New York: Teachers College Press.

Durkin, D. 1979. "What classroom observations reveal about reading comprehension." *Reading Research Quarterly*, 14: 481–533.

Dykstra, D. 1991. E-mail message. XLCHC, 15 April 1991.

Dyson, A. Haas. 1987. *Unintentional helping in the primary grades: Writing in the children's world*. Technical Report No. 2. Center for the Study of Writing. Berkeley, CA.: University of California at Berkeley and Carnegie Mellon University.

Edelsky, C. 1986. *Writing in a bilingual program: Habia una vez*. Norwood, NJ: Ablex.

Edwards, A.D. 1992. "Language, power and cultural identity." In K. Norman, ed. *Thinking voices: The work of the National Oracy Project*. London: Hodder & Stoughton, for the National Curriculum Council.

Edwards, D. 1990. "But what do children really think? Discourse analysis and conceptual content in children's talk." Paper presented at the conference on "Social Interaction and the Acquisition of Knowledge", Universita di Roma, "La Sapienza", Rome, 4–7 December, 1990.

Edwards, D. and N. Mercer. 1987. *Common knowledge*. London: Routledge.

Elliott, J. 1991. *Action research for educational change*. Milton Keynes, U.K.: Open University Press.

Ferreiro, E. 1986. "The interplay between information and assimilation in beginning literacy." In W.H. Teale and E. Sulzby, eds. *Emergent literacy: Writing and reading*. Norwood, NJ: Ablex.

Ferreiro, E. and A. Teberosky. 1982. *Literacy before schooling*. Portsmouth, NH: Heinemann.

Flower, L. 1987. "Interpretive acts: Cognition and the construction of discourse." *Poetics*, 16: 109–30.

Flower, L. and J.R. Hayes. 1981. "A cognitive process theory of writing." *College Composition and Communication*, 32 (4): 365–87.

Forman, E., N. Minick, and A. Stone, eds. In press. *Contexts for learning: Sociocultural dynamics in children's development*. New York: Oxford University Press.

Frankland Inquiry Group (Blake, M., L. Hart-Hewins, M. Kelley, and B. Singleton). 1989. *"Partners in collaborative inquiry and curriculum change: a school-wide buddy reading programme as the vehicle for collaboration among children, teachers, librarians, parents, administrators, and researchers.*" Unpublished report to the Toronto Board of Education. In M. Blake, G.L. Chang, and G. Wells, eds. 1991. *Language and learning: Learners, teachers and researchers at work.* Volume 4: *Collaborative research.* Toronto: Ontario Ministry of Education.

Freedman, S.W., ed. 1985. *The acquisition of written language: Response and revision.* Norwood, NJ: Ablex.

Fullan, M. 1982. *The meaning of educational change.* New York: Teachers' College Press.

Goelman, H., A. Oberg, and F. Smith, eds. 1984. *Awakening to literacy.* Portsmouth, NH: Heinemann.

Goodman, Y. 1980. "The roots of literacy." *Claremont Reading Conference Yearbook,* 44: 1–32.

———. 1984. "The development of initial literacy." In H. Goelman, A. Oberg, and F. Smith, eds. *Awakening to literacy.* Portsmouth, NH: Heinemann.

Goody, J. 1968. *Literacy in traditional societies.* Cambridge: Cambridge University Press.

———. 1977. *The domestication of the savage mind.* Cambridge: Cambridge University Press.

Goswami, D. and P.R. Stillman, eds. 1987. *Reclaiming the classroom: Teacher research as an agency for change.* Portsmouth, NH: Boynton/ Cook-Heinemann.

Hall, N. 1987. *The emergence of literacy.* London: Hodder and Stoughton.

Halliday, M.A.K. 1975. *Learning how to mean.* London: Arnold.

———. 1985. *Spoken and written language.* Geelong, Vic: Deakin University Press. Republished by Oxford University Press, 1989.

Halliday, M.A.K. and R. Hasan. 1985. *Language, context, and text: Aspects of language in a social-semiotic perspective.* Geelong, Vic: Deakin University Press. Republished by Oxford University Press, 1989.

Hammersley, M. 1977. "School learning: The cultural resources required by pupils to answer a teacher's question." In P. Woods and M. Hammersley, eds. *School experience: Explorations in the sociology of education.* London: Croom Helm.

———. 1981. "Putting competence into action: Some sociological notes on a model of classroom interaction." In P. French and M. MacLure, eds. *Adult-Child conversation: Studies in structure and process.* London: Croom Helm.

Heap, J.L. 1985. "Discourse in the production of classroom knowledge." *Curriculum Inquiry,* 15 (3): 245–79.

———. 1986. "Sociality and cognition in collaborative computer writing."

Discussion Paper at the Conference on Literacy and Culture in Educational Settings. Michigan: University of Michigan. 7–9 March 1986.

Heath, S.B. 1983a. "Protean shapes in literacy events: Ever-shifting oral and literate traditions." In D.R. Olson, N. Torrance, and A. Hildyard, eds. *Literacy, language, and learning.* Cambridge: Cambridge University Press.

―――. 1983b. *Ways with words.* Cambridge: Cambridge University Press.

―――. 1986. "Sociocultural contexts of language development." In *Beyond language: Social and cultural factors in schooling language minority students.* Los Angeles, CA: Evaluation, Dissemination and Assessment Center, California State University, Los Angeles.

Hirsch, E.D. 1987. *Cultural literacy: What literate Americans know.* Boston: Houghton Mifflin.

Jaggar, A. and M.T. Smith-Burke, eds. 1985. *Observing the language learner.* Newark, DE: International Reading Association.

Johnson, D.W. and R.T. Johnson. 1990. "Cooperative learning and achievement." In S. Sharan, ed. *Cooperative learning: Theory and research.* New York: Praeger.

Karmiloff-Smith, A. 1979. "Micro- and macro-developmental changes in language acquisition and other representational systems." *Cognitive Science*, 3: 91–118.

Lampert, M. 1989. "Choosing and using mathematical tools in classroom discourse." In J. Brophy, ed. *Advances in research on teaching*, Vol. 1. Greenwich, CT: JAI Press, Inc.

Langer, J.A. 1986. *Children reading and writing: structures and strategies.* Norwood, NJ: Ablex.

―――. 1987. "A sociocognitive perspective on literacy." In J. Langer, ed. *Language, literacy, and culture: Issues of society and schooling.* Norwood, NJ: Ablex.

Lemke, J. 1990. *Talking science.* Norwood, NJ: Ablex.

Lightfoot, M. and N. Martin, eds. *The word for teaching is learning: Essays for James Britton.* London: Heinemann.

Lotman, Y.M. 1988. "Text within a text." *Soviet Psychology*, 26 (3): 32–51.

Luke, A., S. de Castell and C. Luke. 1983. "Beyond criticism: The authority of the school text." *Curriculum Inquiry*, 13: 111–27.

Maher, A. 1991. "Revising my ideas about revision." In M. Blake, G.L. Chang, and G. Wells, eds. 1991. *Language and learning: Learners, teachers and researchers at work.* Volume 4: *Collaborative research.* Toronto: Ontario Ministry of Education.

Martin, J.R. 1984. Language, register and genre. In F. Christie ed. *Children Writing: Reader.* Geelong, Vic: Deakin University Press.

Mead, G.H. 1934. *Mind, self and society.* Chicago: University of Chicago Press.

Mehan, H. 1979. *Learning lessons: Social organization in the classroom.* Cambridge: Harvard University Press.

Moll, L.C., ed. 1990. *Vygotsky and education: Instructional implications and applications of sociohistorical psychology.* Cambridge: Cambridge University Press.

Morrison, K. 1987. "Stabilizing the text: The institutionalization of knowledge in historical and philosophic forms of argument." *Canadian Journal of Sociology,* 12 (3): 242–74.

Murray, D.M. 1978. "Internal revision: A process of discovery." In C.R. Cooper and L. Odell, eds. *Research on composing.* Urbana, IL: National Council of Teachers of English.

———. 1982. *Learning by teaching: Selected articles on writing and teaching.* Portsmouth, NH: Boynton/Cook-Heinemann.

Newman, D., P. Griffin and M. Cole. 1989. *The construction zone: Working for cognitive change in school.* Cambridge: Cambridge University Press.

Newman, J.M. 1987. "Learning to teach by uncovering our assumptions." *Language Arts,* 64 (7): 727–37.

———, ed. 1985. *Whole language: Theory in use.* Portsmouth, NH: Heinemann.

Newson, J. 1978. "Dialogue and development." In A. Lock, ed. *Action, gesture and symbol: The emergence of language.* New York: Academic Press.

Norman, K., ed. 1992. *Thinking voices: The work of the National Oracy Project.* London: Hodder & Stoughton, for the National Curriculum Council.

Ochs, E. 1979. "Transcription as theory." In E. Ochs and B.B. Schieffelin, eds. *Developmental Pragmatics.* New York: Academic Press.

Olson, D.R. 1977. "From utterance to text: The bias of language in speech and writing." *Harvard Educational Review,* 47: 257–81.

———. 1980. "On the language and authority of textbooks." *Journal of Communication,* 30: 186–96.

———. 1986. "The cognitive consequences of literacy." *Canadian Psychology,* 27: 109–21.

Olson, D.R. and J.W. Astington. 1990. "Talking about text: How literacy contributes to thought." *Journal of Pragmatics,* 14: 557–573.

Ong, W. 1982. *Orality and literacy.* New York: Methuen.

Ontario Science Center. 1984. *Scienceworks.* Toronto: Kids Can Press.

Orzechowska, E. and A. Smieja. Forthcoming. "E.S.L. learners talking and thinking in their first language." In G. Wells, ed. *Changing schools from within* (provisional title). Toronto: Joint Centre for Teacher Development, Ontario Institute for Studies in Education.

Painter, C. and J.R. Martin, eds. 1987. *Writing to mean: Teaching genres across the curriculum.* Occasional paper. The Applied Linguistics Association of Australia.

Palincsar, A.S. and A.L. Brown. 1984. "Reciprocal teaching of compre-
hension-fostering and comprehension-monitoring activities." *Cognition
and Instruction*, 1 (2): 117–75.

Pascual-Leone, J. 1980. "Constructive problems for constructive theories:
The current relevance of Piaget's work and a critique of information-
processing simulation psychology." In R. H. Klume and H. Spada, eds.
Developmental Models of Thinking. New York: Academic Press.

Piaget, J. 1977. *The development of thought: Equilibrium of cognitive
structures.* A. Rosin, trans. New York: Viking.

Piaget, J. and B. Inhelder. 1969. *The psychology of the child.* New York:
Basic Books.

Pinnell, G.S. and M.L. Matlin, eds. 1989. *Teachers and research: Language
learning in the classroom.* Newark, DE: International Reading
Association.

Plowden, Lady B. 1967. *Children and their primary schools.* London:
H.M. Stationery Office.

Rogoff, B. 1990. *Apprenticeship in thinking.* New York: Oxford University
Press.

Rogoff, B. and J. Lave, eds. 1984. *Everyday cognition: Its development in
social context.* Cambridge: Harvard University Press.

Rogoff, B., C. Mosier, J. Mistry, and A. Goncu. Forthcoming. "Toddlers'
guided participation in cultural activity." To appear in J. Wertsch, ed.
Cultural dynamics.

Rommetveit, R. 1985. Language acquisition as increasing linguistic structuring of experience and symbolic behavior control. In J. Wertsch
ed. *Culture, communication and cognition: Vygotskian perspectives.*
New York: Cambridge University Press.

Rosen, C. and H. Rosen 1973. *The language of primary school children.*
Harmondsworth, Middlesex: Penguin.

Rosenblatt, L. 1988. *Writing and reading: The transactional theory.* Center
for the Study of Writing, Technical Report No. 13. University of
California at Berkeley and Carnegie Mellon University.

Scardamalia, M. and C. Bereiter. 1985. "Development of dialectical processes
in composition." In D. Olson, N. Torrance, and A. Hildyard, eds.
*Literacy, language and learning: The nature and consequences of
reading and writing.* Cambridge: Cambridge University Press.

Schaffer, H.R. 1977. "Early interactive development." In H.R. Schaffer, ed.
Studies in mother-infant interaction. London: Academic Press.

Schaefer, R.J. 1967. *The school as a center of inquiry.* New York: Harper
and Row.

Schieffelin, B.B. 1987. "Literacy in multiethnic and multicultural contexts:
Introduction." In D.A. Wagner, ed. *The future of literacy in a changing
world.* New York: Pergamon Press.

Schieffelin, B.B. and M. Cochran-Smith. 1984. Learning to read culturally:
Literacy before schooling. In H. Goelman, A. Oberg, and F. Smith, eds.

Awakening to literacy. Portsmouth, NH: Heinemann.

Schön, D. 1983. *The reflective practitioner: How professionals think in action.* New York: Basic Books.

Scribner, S. and M. Cole. 1981. *The psychology of literacy.* Cambridge: Harvard University Press.

Service, R. 1986. The cremation of Sam McGee. Toronto: Kids Can Press.

Sharan, S. and Y. Sharan. 1976. *Small group teaching.* Englewood Cliffs, NJ: Educational Technology Publications.

Shechter, M. and B. Singleton. In press. "Genre-based whole language programmes: teacher, researcher and student perspectives." In M. Blake, G.L. Chang, and G. Wells, eds. 1991. *Language and learning: Learners, teachers and researchers at work.* Volume 4: *Collaborative research.* Toronto: Ontario Ministry of Education.

Sinclair, J.M. and R.M. Coulthard. 1975. *Towards an analysis of discourse: The English used by teachers and pupils.* London: Oxford University Press.

Smith, F. 1983. *Essays into literacy.* Portsmouth, NH: Heinemann.

Stenhouse, L. 1975. *An introduction to curriculum research and development.* London: Heinemann.

Stock. B. 1983. *The implications of literacy.* Princeton: Princeton University Press.

Street, B.V. 1987. "Literacy and social change: The significance of social context in the development of literacy programmes." In D.A. Wagner, ed. *The future of literacy in a changing world.* New York: Pergamon Press.

Sulzby, E. and W.H. Teale. 1987. *Young children's storybook reading: Longitudinal study of parent-child interaction and children's independent functioning.* Final Report to the Spencer Foundation. Ann Arbor: The University of Michigan.

Tannen, D. 1985. "Relative focus on involvement in oral and written discourse." In D. Olson, N. Torrance, and A. Hildyard, eds. *Literacy, language and learning.* Cambridge: Cambridge University Press.

———. 1989. *Talking voices: Repetition, dialogue, and imagery in conversational discourse.* Cambridge: Cambridge University Press.

Taylor, D. 1983. *Family literacy: Young children learning to read and write.* Portsmouth, NH: Heinemann.

Teale, W.H. 1984. "Reading to young children: Its significance for literacy development." In H. Goelman, A. Oberg, and F. Smith, eds. *Awakening to literacy.* Portsmouth, NH: Heineman.

———. 1986. "Home background and young children's literacy development." In W.H. Teale and E. Sulzby, eds. *Emergent literacy: Writing and reading.* Norwood, NJ: Ablex.

Tharp, R. and R. Gallimore. 1988. *Rousing minds of life.* Cambridge: Cambridge University Press.

Tizard, B. and M. Hughes. 1984. *Young children learning: Talking and thinking at home and at school.* London: Fontana.

Vygotsky, L.S. 1956. *Izbrannie psikhologicheskie issledovaniya.* [Selected psychological research.] Moscow: Izdatel'stvo Akademii Pedagogicheskikh Nauk.

———. 1962. *Thought and language.* Cambridge: M.I.T. Press.

———. 1978. *Mind in society.* Cambridge: Harvard University Press.

———. 1981. "The genesis of higher mental functions." In J. Wertsch, ed. *The concept of activity in Soviet psychology.* Armonk, NY: Sharpe Inc.

Wells, G. 1985a. *Language development in the pre-school years.* Cambridge: Cambridge University Press.

———. 1985b. *Language, learning and education.* Windsor, U.K. NFER-Nelson.

———. 1986. *The meaning makers: Children learning language and using language to learn.* Portsmouth, NH: Heinemann.

———. 1987. "Apprenticeship in literacy." *Interchange*, 18 [1/2]: 109–23.

———. 1990. "Intersubjectivity and the construction of knowledge." Paper presented at the conference on Social Interaction and the Acquisition of Knowledge, Universita di Roma, "La Sapienza", Rome, 4–7 December 1990.

———, ed. Forthcoming. *Changing schools from within.* (provisional title) Toronto: Joint Centre for Teacher Development, Ontario Institute for Studies in Education.

Wells, G. and G.L. Chang. 1986. "From speech to writing: Some evidence on the relationship between oracy and literacy." In A. Wilkinson, ed. *The writing of writing.* Milton Keynes, U.K.: Open University Press.

Wertsch, J.V. ed. 1981. *The concept of activity in Soviet psychology.* Armonk, NY: Sharpe Inc.

———, ed. 1985a. *Culture, communication, and cognition: Vygotskian perspectives.* Cambridge: Cambridge University Press.

———. 1985b. *Vygotsky and the social formation of mind.* Cambridge: Harvard University Press.

———. 1991. *Voices of the mind.* Cambridge: Harvard University Press.

Wertsch, J.V. and C.A. Stone. 1985. "The concept of internalization in Vygotsky's account of the genesis of higher mental functions." In J.V. Wertsch ed. *Culture, communication, and cognition: Vygotskian perspectives* Cambridge: Cambridge University Press.

Wertsch, J.V. and Toma. 1990. "Discourse and learning in the classroom: A sociocultural approach." Worcester, MA: Frances L. Hiatt School of Psychology, Clark University. Unpublished paper.

Wittrock, M.C. 1974. "Learning as a generative process." *Educational Psychologist*, 11: 87–95.

Wood, D. 1988. *How children think and learn.* Oxford: Blackwell.

Index